Spiritual Mountaineering

Copyright © 2020 Jim Monsor

JAM Publishing

All rights reserved. No part of this book may be reproduced or transmitted in any form or by any means (electronic or mechanical, including photocopying, recording, or by any information storage and retrieval system) without written permission from the author — except for brief quotations in book reviews.

Unless otherwise noted, all scripture quotations taken from the New American Standard Bible®, Copyright © 1960, 1962, 1963, 1968, 1971, 1972, 1973, 1975, 1977, 1995 by The Lockman Foundation Used by permission. (www.Lockman.org)

ISBN: 978-1-7325420-6-8
ISBN: 978-1-7325420-7-5 (e-book)

Cover and interior design: Bill Kersey, KerseyGraphics

Printed in the United States of America

Spiritual
Mountaineering

Climbing the Mountains of God

Jim Monsor

JAM Publishing

DEDICATION

....

Beth Monsor is not only my beautiful and loving wife, but she has seen me through my entire adult life journey. Aside from Christ, she has impacted who I am far more than anyone. I couldn't be more grateful for and to her. Beth, I dedicate this book to you.

ENDORSEMENTS

....

"As a mountain climber, Jim Monsor knows the training, discipline, teamwork, risks, and rewards of summiting the great peaks. I was there when Jim spoke at our church men's retreat on "Spiritual Mountaineering." He helped us see the path to a more serious and vibrant faith, the kind that gets people off the couch and away from cell phones—to actually conquer obstacles, to strain, and to finally stand in that rare and thrilling zone of the Presence of God. Jim has now carried that same challenging and inspiring view into these pages. This is the book that could finally pull you from the zones of comfort and up over the top!"

Michael W. Smith, Singer/Songwriter

"There has never been a more important time to encourage people toward a dynamic personal relationship with Jesus Christ. What is refreshingly unique about *Spiritual Mountaineering*, is that Jim Monsor has given us a complete template for spiritual growth. He skillfully uses his personal story of mountain climbing to give us practical and accessible pathways toward intimacy with God and personal success.

"The insights he draws from his experience are profound and readily applicable to the rigors of daily life. This is not an abstract discipleship system; he gives real-life experiences with real-life answers anchored in timeless biblical truth. I highly recommend *Spiritual Mountaineering* for personal development and for small group study and business coaching."

STEVE FRY
President, Messenger Fellowship and Senior Pastor, Gate Community Church

"Our world needs more strong men that lead with vulnerability. Jim takes the time to share his personal journey and delivers a wealth of insight into our challenges and struggles. If you are looking for clarity on how to navigate life and understand your purpose, this book will speak to you.

"There are no silver bullets in life, but for me, reading this book was like sitting down with a wise and trusted mentor. I gleaned some of critically important truths about leadership and manhood. Just like the crisp and clear perspective from the top of a peak, this book refreshed and reminded me that life is an epic journey and that there truly is *more*."

BRIAN JOBE
COO of Church on the Move and cofounder of Mountain Men

"Jim Monsor's fine book, *Spiritual Mountaineering*, grew from a seed the Spirit planted over twenty years ago with students at the University of Texas. I remember the students' excitement about climbing higher in the Kingdom of God. I believe this book will catch fire in hearts again. I pray many will hear the Lord's voice in this book and be challenged to climb higher in our Lord!"

VICTOR SCHOBER
Former Executive Presbyter and District Superintendent,
North Texas District, Assemblies of God

"Godly discipline, according to Hebrews 12:10, leads to our sharing in the holiness of God. Reaching God's high country is never easy. It takes great discipline. But it produces a harvest of righteousness and peace for those who have been trained by it.

Spiritual Mountaineering is a blueprint for translating that truth into real-life experience. Jim Monsor, in facing many mountains in his lifetime, has learned the value and rewards of discipline and perseverance.

"My hope and my prayer for every seeker of true adventure and purpose in life is that they will read this book thoroughly and honestly. If they do, they'll **never be the same.** This is a modern-day blueprint outline graphically shared at a personal level that explains God's ancient promise to the lives of those who kept pressing **on** and **in** and **through**."

REV. DR. ALISTAIR PETRIE
Pastor, Author, and
Executive Director of Partnership Ministries
www.partnershipministries.org

"I'm grateful Jim Monsor has responded to God's call to write this book. Through the preparation and journey to the summit, Jim inspires us to move beyond the truth of who Christ is and do the hard work of walking more fully alive in our faith. I'm grateful for the challenging moments I have spent digging into my own walk as a result."

RICK STEINBERGER
Board Advisor, Young Life

"Adventure is surely one of humanity's greatest needs; it speaks to discovery, exploration, risk, invitation, learning, and perseverance. We find adventure in every aspect of daily life. Hearing a sound of Christ's Kingdom and responding is no doubt the greatest adventure any of us will experience. Exploring this Kingdom is a lifelong expedition where we find identity, belonging, and purpose—wisdom for the really big questions!

"I've learned mountaineering is a lens through which to see spiritual life. I know readers will find themselves caught up in the adventure their heart has yearned for. I invite you to explore Jim Monsor's *Spiritual Mountaineering* as he shares joys, struggles, and triumphs from his journey. This book presents this clarion call for Kingdom adventure. Enjoy every step!"

MARK DUGGIN
Lifechangers, Inc. CEO and mountaineer

APPRECIATION

....

This book would not have been possible without the help and support of so many others. Vic Schober, who invested so much in me. Ed Chinn, who never let me off easy throughout the writing and editing process. My four daughters—Ann, Claire, Megan, and Kate—who have been such a pivotal anchor in my life. Mark Duggin and Alex Van Steen, who gave me such valuable insight from a mountaineer's perspective. All of the people who are my Base Camp and praying for me and my company on a regular basis. I thank you all. You have helped shape who I am.

I also thank those who read the manuscript, sometimes repeatedly. You each made it stronger and clearer than it would have been without you. So, thank you, Steve Fry, Michael W. Smith, Tom Bates, Terry Blankenship, Chip Bratten, Len Harrison, Suzanne Stroud, Alistair Petrie, Todd Bruinsma, Zane Browning, Erik Eskelund, Pam Godwin, Erik Hilder, Aaron Weaver, Chad Hardcastle, Ann Monsor, Brian Jobe, Caleb Phillips, Stan Moser, John Sommers, and Rick Steinberger.

PREFACE

....

I HAVE ALWAYS HOPED FOR SOMETHING MORE FROM LIFE THAN putting in my 85-ish years, raising kids, and pursuing success. A sense of something bigger has always called out to me. At various times, it seemed to tease or tug at me from somewhere "out there." But, for most of my life, that something bigger seemed just beyond my view or reach.

When I became a Christian, it became a bit clearer: I did not arrive here on my own or by accident. God made me and placed me; He has a plan. Therefore, I've driven hard, pedal-to-the-floor, to maximize my potential in every way so that when God is ready to use me, He can say "Now I've got something I can work with."

All of that is probably why I've been drawn to the outdoors all my life. Something always compelled me to reach for the raw and beautiful nature of this earth. That may be why, as a young man, I became fascinated with mountains. Throughout my years, I have read most of the literature about Everest climbs.

In 2002, in my early 40s, I climbed Mount Rainier. By that time, I had attained significant success in my career and in our church. Something about stepping from the corporate and church worlds into mountaineering changed me. Deeply. The very real world of mountain climbing nailed two things for me:

1. It revived my dreams of (and search for) a life with meaning, passion, and impact. Standing at the summit, taking in the indescribable beauty and perfection of God convinced me He wanted more from my life.
2. It caused me to see how Christian culture trivializes the very real and awesome experience of walking with God. We are too often just not serious about our life in Him.

Now, at 61, I more clearly see how the natural realm of mountaineering can help us to better understand God's transcendent ways, purposes, and plans.

What about you?

You didn't stumble into your life either. God also made and placed you according to His good pleasure. Yes, He has a plan; and it is larger than you ever dreamed.

Could God be calling you to higher ground?

TABLE *of* CONTENTS

....

PART 1
WHY MOUNTAINS MATTER

CHAPTER 1: **A Very Personal Mountain**..........................19

CHAPTER 2: **Climb!** 25

CHAPTER 3: **A Mountain Called** 29

CHAPTER 4: **Above the Clouds** 35

CHAPTER 5: **Higher Ground** 39

PART 2
MESSAGES FROM THE MOUNTAINS

CHAPTER 6: **What is the Mountain?**..............................45

CHAPTER 7: **Training and Preparation for the Climb** 53

CHAPTER 8: **What's in Your Pack?** 63

CHAPTER 9: **Who's on Your Team?** 71

CHAPTER 10: **Planning Your Route** 85

CHAPTER 11: **The Way of the Mountaineer** 91

CHAPTER 12: **Focus on the Goal** 105

CHAPTER 13: **Understand the Dangers and Risks** 117

CHAPTER 14: **Mountain Rescue and Response** 125

PART 3
LEAVING A LEGACY

CHAPTER 15: **A Heart for Unnamed Peaks** 135

CHAPTER 16: **The Heart of the Mountaineer** 139

APPENDICES 149

AUTHOR BIO 155

Part 1

....

WHY MOUNTAINS MATTER

"The ethereal rise of a ridge in mist, the glint of moonlight on an icy face, a flare of gold on a distant peak – such glimpses of transcendent beauty can reveal our world as a place of unimaginable mystery and splendor. In the fierce play of natural elements that swirl about their summits – thunder, lightning, wind, and clouds – mountains also embody powerful forces beyond our control, physical expressions of an awesome reality that can overwhelm us with feelings of wonder and fear."

– Ed Bernbaum

Sacred Mountains of the World (Random House, 1990)

What is it about mountains or mountain ranges that so captivates our attention? At the simplest level, mountains are dominant geological features. They surpass; they simply rise above the normal landscapes. The sheer elevation demands that we look.

Although we walk, run, or dance across flat land, to ascend a mountain requires determination, exertion, and focus. That alone separates climbers from everyone else. It's called "resistance." Level ground accommodates our bodies, but mountains fight back. They often discourage, sometimes they injure, and they also kill. Mountaineering is war. You have to battle your own mind and body in order to rise *up*. Then, whether you cross them like Lewis and Clark crossed the Bitterroot Range or summit them like Sir Edmund Hillary conquered Mount Everest, you have to *overcome* mountains.

But, mountains reward those who persevere. The summit grants a view that most people never see. The rare atmosphere gives new heights of clarity, insight, and awe. In that sense, mountains are metaphors. That's probably why struggles with illness, injury, and insufficiency often find the language of mountaineering to be the best and most accurate vocabulary for the story.

That's why we are so drawn to them.

I have climbed mountains, geologically and metaphorically; I know what it is to summit a great peak. And I also know what it is to press upward, cry, bleed, and fall.

This book captures my story. But, it's also your story. Everyone faces a mountain at some point. You know yours, but maybe you need a guide. I've crossed the jagged terrain ahead many times. I want to help you cross yours and summit your Everest.

CHAPTER 1

A VERY PERSONAL MOUNTAIN

....

*I*NEVER THOUGHT IT WOULD TAKE 60 YEARS TO GET TO MY mountain. I always felt that somewhere in my late 40s to mid- 50s I would really hit my stride. And in a lot of respects, I did. But the really clear picture of my mountain didn't come into view until I was nearly 60. And even now, I'm not sure I see all of it. But I have finally arrived at Base Camp (more on that in the chapters ahead), and I have never been more excited about the climb ahead in my life. Most people have no idea how new biomedical products or medical equipment inventions find their way into existence. I do. I understand the astronomical investment, the years of research, the yards gained and lost, the intrigue, and the pallets of documentation shipped to the FDA. That work probably shaped my view of mountaineering.

The risks of failure in pharmaceutical development can be frightening, even crushing. Those who work in my world know the risk of the whole dream blowing up. That is just as true of a big company as it is of small startups. Early in my career, I worked on a multi-billion-dollar investment for a major pharmaceutical company. After ten years of development and massive investments, a few patients died in a late-stage clinical trial. As tragic as their deaths were, they were all "at-risk" patients; all suffered significant complicating factors that could have caused their deaths. Staring death in the face is undoubtedly why they volunteered for the trial. But it didn't matter, the company cut the program completely. Several hundred people lost their jobs overnight. All the security we thought we had in the large company evaporated. Everyone had just a few months to find new positions. To work in the biomedical arena is to live on the razor's edge.

The world of biomedical science has been my business for several decades. But, the path to get here was not easy or straightforward. For example, I endured a forced and prolonged "vacation" of 13 long months in 2001-2002, while living in Austin, Texas. I was between jobs and it was just one of those times when no career or investment opportunities seemed right for me. But, during that window, I met Bob Hofmann, an ophthalmologist who had developed a novel pharmaceutical product in the late 1990s. Strangely, while attending a Pentecostal prayer meeting with a friend, a woman "prophesied" over him: "You carry '*disruptive innovation*.'" And, that was at least 10 years before Clayton Christensen coined the term.

Very early studies with his product treating Dry Form Macular Degeneration, a neurodegenerative disorder similar to Parkinson's, melanoma, lymphoma, and mast cell cancer in dogs, had shown astonishing results. So, he raised funding and assembled a small team. I joined the team to help drive the development work necessary for FDA approval.

Nine months later we moved to Nashville, where I became part of the leadership team for a biotech startup. After leaving Bob's team,

I lost touch with him. Over the years, I often thought of him and our work together, wondering if and how that all fit into the grand scheme of my career progression. But I was consumed with driving the new company to success, so the question just drifted into the background.

The new biotech company was very successful. Our small team achieved FDA approval on a first-in-class device/biologic combination product (essentially a bone regeneration system) in less than four and half years. That was a truly remarkable accomplishment for a very novel, very elegant product. We went through an IPO, introduced other products in the platform, and were ultimately acquired by a larger company in 2013. I left the company a year later.

After a couple of years of searching for the path into the next career gig, two other colleagues and I founded Relay Life Science in 2016. We handle the middle "legs of the relay race" for life science technology development between the research and commercialization (the "valley of death").[1] We develop pharmaceutical, medical device, and animal health technologies to the point where a large pharmaceutical or medical device company may become interested in buying them. Rather than developing companies that are acquired, we develop *products* that the acquirers can easily integrate into their commercial operations.

A Change in Elevation

In 2015 I began noticing some odd neurological issues with my left hand. I wondered if I might have had a minor stroke. But it wasn't a significant impairment so I kind of ignored it. Then in 2016, I lost the

---

1 That is the period between early research to define a product concept and the time when data will attract investment. It's called "valley of death" because it's the time when innovators desperately need capital but cannot attract it.

ability to type with my left hand. Although I had always been able to type quickly, I found myself staring at my left hand, thinking "come on...*move*! What's going on here?" After six months of chiropractic care, followed by six months of physical therapy under the direction of a spine specialist, I saw no change. I did not know what was going on, but I knew something had changed. I had to exert more energy to do what I had always done very easily. Everything seemed like an uphill push.

In early 2017, Vanderbilt neurologists reviewed my medical records and said they could not see me until January 2018. Since they didn't seem to see any urgency, I thought it probably wasn't a serious issue. But, as a precautionary measure, my spine doc called for an MRI on my brain and brain stem to rule out stroke or tumors. The morning before my MRI, my wife Beth saw a Facebook post about a researcher at the Barrow Institute in Phoenix who had just received a large grant to develop a more precise high-resolution MRI. We didn't think much more about it. And my MRI results came through clean, no stroke or tumors. But, a few days later, we shared the MRI results and the Vanderbilt feedback with our Sunday School class. Didn't mention anything else.

A friend in the class, a physician who had just retired from a senior executive position with Hospital Corporation of America, spoke up: "I don't think you know this, but before I moved to Nashville I was at the Barrow Institute in Phoenix; I can probably get you an appointment there in a few weeks."

About that same time (March of 2018) I once again began wondering what ever happened with Bob Hofmann's product. I wondered if my company could be a means of developing his technology. I tried reaching him via email, phone, LinkedIn, nothing, no response. So, I shrugged it off.

The Missing Piece

Two weeks before going out to Phoenix, I attended an investor conference in Washington, DC. On two of the evenings, I met with some friends who were central figures in Capitol Hill prayer initiatives. Near the end of our prayer time, one of them said to me: "You're a vessel like a coffee mug or pitcher that is missing a piece. That piece is the handle. When that piece falls in place, God can pick you up and use you in more profound ways than ever before." It intrigued me but I didn't really know what to make of it, so I thanked him and said I'd keep my eyes and ears open.

In late May, Beth and I walked into The Muhammad Ali Movement Disorders Clinic at the Barrow Institute. Our appointment started promptly at 7:00 a.m. After a 20-minute evaluation, the doctor announced that I had Parkinson's Disease. Boom, just like that. Beth, naturally, went through the typical shock/recoil process.

But my mind was somewhere else. As soon as I heard "Parkinson's," I heard a clear and almost-audible voice, "This is the missing piece."

CHAPTER 2

CLIMB!

....

When we got back to our hotel room, Beth had to get some alone time. Quite naturally, she was still processing through the shock and recoil. But I hit the ground running. It suddenly became more important to find Bob Hofmann. So, after scouring the internet, including social media, I finally found an obscure email address for him. Although I wasn't sure it was current, I sent him a quick email.

He responded almost immediately. Told me he was living in New Zealand and practicing again as an ophthalmologist. Then he updated me about the 16 years since I left the company. After hitting product development roadblocks and running through all their capital, Bob lost hope and left that company. In September 2007, he signed a settlement agreement with his former partners, including a 10-year non-compete agreement. But, by the time we reconnected, all the patents had expired. Furthermore, at the time of our email, Bob held an entirely new molecule design with a completely different manufacturing process. And, in three months his non-compete agreement would expire, and we could start working together again.

Two weeks after our return from Phoenix, Beth and I attended a church meeting that gathered about 15 people, including a few speakers. When one speaker finished, she asked if anyone would like prayer. Beth and I stood. And, she bore into me like no one ever had before. Among other things, she said: "You are broad and supposed to be broad. Why do you think you've gotten so excited recently? Something's coming, that you were made for. You're not all over the place. He says you're wide and you're meant to be wide. You carry disruptive innovation, both in the Kingdom and the Marketplace... And the Lord says: 'I won't waste you.' You're going to step into what you saw years ago... And there is a part of you that says 'It's too scary to hope and believe that this is it.' This is it, you're almost there. Don't give up now. Do not let the delayed promise bring frustration."

She had no way of knowing about my diagnosis or my reconnection with Bob.

A month later, Bob filled in some more details when he told me he had continued to pursue the R and D of his molecule. In fact, he had scheduled a presentation for the physicians at his practice, as part of his efforts to raise capital to fund the development of the molecule. My email came in the night before his presentation was scheduled. He canceled the presentation.

Later, Beth reminded me that when I worked with Bob in 2002, I had about 19 years of relevant experience, a few years in very early stage research and about 15 in large- and small-scale commercial operations. But I had relatively little experience in the D of R&D (Research and Development) and then pre-clinical development, clinical trial execution, and the "valley of death." I gained *that* experience in the 16 years since I had worked with Bob. So, I wasn't even qualified to lead the commercial development of Bob's compounds back in 2002. But now, I am uniquely qualified to do that.

So, with the concurrent Parkinson's diagnosis and the greatest business challenge of my life, I have come to clearly see the mountain that lies ahead of me. It is that massive topography that stands between me and my purpose. As I wrote earlier, you have your own mountain. But, whether it is mine or yours, I can assure you that there is no way around it; the only path to the other side goes right over the summit.

As I've climbed this mountain of Parkinson's and my new business venture, my mind has traveled back to another time and another mountain. August, 2002, Mount Rainier.

CHAPTER 3

A MOUNTAIN CALLED

....

I STUMBLED ONTO THE PLANE IN SEATTLE JUST AFTER 9 P.M. AND found a seat in the rear. I fell sound asleep before the plane even pushed back from the gate.

Twenty-one hours earlier, after a few hours of restless sleep, the guides woke us at midnight. We were back on the climb in less than 45 minutes. Leaving the 10,000-foot climber's hut, the plan was to make the 14,410-foot summit of Mount Rainier in less than nine hours. This was, after all, why we were on the mountain. Some of us had trained for more than nine months for that day. Rainier is not the highest peak in the US, but it is the highest in the Cascade Range. It is also one of the most dangerous peaks in the world. About 60 people have died on Rainier. And that number climbs each year.

Just before 1:00 a.m., our three small climbing teams headed up the mountain. We wore full mountaineering gear, including climber's helmets with lamps, boots, crampons, and an ice axe. The bobbing and weaving shafts of light from our headlamps sliced through the darkness, partially illuminating the narrow path up the steep slope of ice and rock.

Over the first four hours of pushing our way up the steep upper slopes of Rainier, the eastern sky began to lighten. Black rolled to gray to indigo to blue to breaking dawn. Four more hours of grinding the steep slopes of the volcanic cone in early morning light brought us to the top of Washington State. After pushing our bodies well beyond what most of us thought we could endure, we stood at the 14,410-foot summit of Mount Rainier.

At that moment, we occupied a place higher than any other humans in the great northwest. From that soaring peak I could see, in one stunning sweep, most of the Cascade Range, from Canada to Mount Hood and even Mount Jefferson down in Oregon. But our time at the summit was brief. Only 30 minutes later, we headed back down. Coming down the mountain was much harder than going up; descending the glacier-capped cone was a continual and grueling resistance to pitching forward down the mountain.

Our lead guide, Alex Van Steen, pushed us down the mountain. Hard. He knew the risks; as the day wore on, the sun was warming the ice, making the icy surface loose and extremely slick. Not only can the climbers lose their footing and fall, but they are also in danger from the climbers above them. A climbing team could fall and hurtle down the slope, shearing everyone below them right off the mountain. So Alex pushed hard; my quadriceps felt on fire. I was certain I would fall.

We covered the 4,400 feet back down to Camp Muir in three hours. After an hour to pack up the gear, we headed back down to Paradise, 5,000 feet on down the mountain. In 15 hours, we traveled about 18 miles and 13,500 feet of vertical terrain.

I was used up, spent; Rainier took all I had. At six-foot-five and a very fit 220 pounds, I was one of the strongest people in the group. But when my 42-year-old body collapsed into the seat at the back of the plane, I was pretty well gone. It proved to be harder than I expected, and it took more out of me than I ever imagined.

But I had climbed the mountain.

August 5, 2002, will always be a very high peak on the range of my life. Mount Rainier called. I answered. That enormous slab of rock, rising almost three miles into the Washington sky, has long been inviting people to its high adventure. The names assigned to its features – Disappointment Cleaver, Liberty Ridge, Cadaver Gap, Success Cleaver – reveal its calls and rewards and risks. The mountain calls and rewards those who press through. But it can also disappoint, break, and kill. Many very able men and women have lost their lives on Rainier.

Yet, many others have faced death and lived to tell the story.

Before my friend, Mark Duggin, climbed Rainier in June 2016, he and his climbing partner, Brad Davidson, took all the normal precautions as seasoned mountaineers. They knew they were ready. The night before their climb, the Rainier climbing rangers told everyone that the next morning appeared to be a good window for summiting. Mark described that window as "gorgeous...picture perfect."[2] So, feeling as prepared as they could be, Mark and Brad started climbing before dawn on June 17. After dropping their backpacks at the edge of the crater rim, they crossed the quarter-mile-wide crater and climbed the last 400 feet to the summit around 8:30 a.m.

That's when the story changed.

---

2 "Two Climbers Survive a Blizzard at 14,000 Feet," CBN, August 3, 2019, https://www1.cbn.com/video/MIR36v4/two-climbers-survive-a-blizzard-at-14-000-feet?show=700club

According to Peter Ellis, a park climbing ranger, the storm barreled up Rainier "shockingly fast."[3] Within minutes, the climbers could not see. But they managed to descend back down to the crater. Their digital compass and GPS unit were frozen and their magnetic compass was in their packs, packs they could not find in the blizzard. As experienced climbers, they knew they faced a very dangerous situation. To survive required their equipment, food, and supplies. And shovels.

But, because of their experience and general maturity, they remained calm. Remembering that they dropped their packs near the other side of the crater rim, they carefully followed the rocky perimeter of the crater until they found the packs. Knowing that descending was impossible from their 14,300-foot location, they sent a distress signal (which the rangers received) and then began digging into the ice and snow to build a shelter.

After seven hours, they carved out what Mark called a "two-person casket." With a tarp thrown over the top, they rode out three days of blizzard conditions, subzero temperatures, and 50-mph winds. For three days, they could not move, except to crawl out to knock the piling snow off the tarp roof. They waited, and they prayed.

On the third day, a Sunday and Father's Day, the weather broke. Mark and Brad started down the mountain. Forty-five minutes later, they saw a park helicopter. The chopper's mission to recover human remains quickly turned into a rescue mission.

Such harrowing stories are also part of the call and mystique of mountains. Even if they've not read him, most mountain climbers instinctively resonate to the words of Sir Frances Younghusband:

---

3 Craig Hill, "How 'smart, tough' climbers survive 2-day storm near top of Mount Rainier," The News Tribune (Tacoma, WA), June 26, 2016

"To those who have struggled with them, the mountains reveal beauties they will not disclose to those who make no effort. That is the reward the mountains give to the effort. And it is because they have so much to give and give it so lavishly to those who will wrestle with them that men love the mountains and go back to them again and again…the mountains reserve their choice gifts for those who stand on their summits."[4]

---

4 Charles Kenneth Howard-Bury, George H. Leigh-Mallory, and A. F. R. Wollaston, *Mount Everest, The Reconnaissance, 1921* (New York: Longman's, Green, and Company, 1922) p. 4 (Sir Frances Younghusband's Introduction)

CHAPTER 4

ABOVE THE CLOUDS

....

My legs were so shot from the climb that for three days after I got home, I could not even walk up a flight of stairs to kiss my kids good night. The climb brought a life-altering impact to me. Just as Moses was changed by what happened on a mountain, I was too. I had crossed over a boundary from an old way of life; I have never seen reality the same since that climb.

I've often wondered, why do mountaineers climb mountains? What is that mysterious call to a mountain? The old cliché, "Because they're there," doesn't come close to answering the question.

Some climb for the sheer exhilaration of it, the pure beauty, the rush of breathing clear, dry air in high places above the clouds, or the raw majesty of the mountains themselves. Those climbers thrive on pushing the limit of their capacity. Many are driven by a passion for the challenge and a remarkable willingness to deal with high risk. Most people cannot fathom that kind of unrelenting single-mindedness.

Successful climbers maintain intense focus in the midst of extreme conditions. They seem to have some distant view, far above the mass of humanity. The mountain climbers I have met all seem to have a deep discontent or disinterest with the stuff of ordinary life, similar to how people who have had near-death experiences view life. These people are not tied to the things of this world, the lesser things of life. With simple humility, they are content with the solitude of the remote wilderness. Something within drives them to be true to the deep rhythms of the heart.

I've also wondered, why did *I* climb a mountain? What was that mysterious call to *my* mountain?

In that Rainier climb, I felt like God picked up the thread He had been weaving for more than 20 years–starting with a fall from a cliff, a word delivered to my heart by a 19-year-old co-worker, a small church in Waukegan, Illinois—and in countless other meetings with Him. He reignited all that on the mountain.

In the mid-90s, when I worked as a mid-level manager at a large pharmaceutical company, God would not leave me alone. He seemed to keep asking me, "What are you here for? When you face the end of your days, looking back over your life, what do you want to see?"

While He spoke to me, I spent hours on my face pleading for insight. "God, what do you want from me? Why did You make me the way I am? Why did You give me this family—these specific people, Beth and our daughters? Why am I so dissatisfied with what most Christians feel is a decent life? What are you doing with me? I need some feedback; I need some answers and direction!" I needed to get above the clouds somehow.

In the end, all my prayers boiled down to a single theme: "God, although I may not know what You are doing or recognize Your shaping of my life…have Your way in me; make me whom You designed me to be." I think that is where the deep yearning began turning to action. I had responded to the call to climb the mountain of God.

Disaster!

In the midst of my time of wrestling with God, a story grabbed me and would not let me go.

May 11, 1996, was the worst day in the history of Mount Everest. Two tourist climbs, led by two of the most experienced high-altitude climbers in the world, were high on the mountain. People had paid big bucks to be led to the top of the world. Members of both teams had made the summit late in the day but had become separated from one another. Many were disoriented due to exposure; they had been in the Death Zone for more than 24 hours, and most had run out of oxygen. When a serious blizzard rolled up the mountain late in the afternoon, laying siege to everything above 23,000 feet, most of the climbers were in whiteout. They lost the use of their arms and legs due to frostbite, exhaustion, and lack of food and water; some were blinded by ice crusting over their eyes. Eight died in a span of 36 hours.

Over the following couple of years, I read at least four accounts of that climb. What captured me most was the challenge for the team leaders and guides to lead groups of relatively inexperienced climbers to the top of the only mountain on earth that pierces the jet stream. It is not the most difficult mountain to climb, but the conditions can be worse than anywhere else on the planet. How did such experienced team leaders allow things to get to the point where two of the best climbers in the world and six other teammates died?

That stirred me. Deeply. What does it mean to be a leader? What does it mean to exercise good judgment when the stakes are really high? What does it mean to achieve real, lasting impact, to lead with excellence, and survive the challenges and risks? What is "greatness"? Why is the climb to "greatness" often such a lonely and risky ascent?

And why have so many leaders, after achieving great success, fallen off the mountain? I could see incredible parallels with the disaster on Everest. How and why did those leaders put themselves in a position where they and their teams could fall and be lost forever? Truly, the responsibility and, therefore, accountability of leadership in any arena is a heavy weight to bear. History confirms that decisions at critical moments can yield profound and far-reaching consequences.

CHAPTER 5

HIGHER GROUND

....

Growing up, I never had much appetite for religious people. Nor did I have any interest in the "Born Again Christian" scene.

But I always thought that there was something more. Something bigger than me. Something about life that was really important, more important than having the perfect American experience of success, 2.5 kids, nice house, expensive stuff....and then death.

Something called from a distant place; it spoke to something deep within me. That Something (or Someone) is what kept me going through my teen years; a time marked by my parent's divorce, my older sister's death at 23 after a two-year battle with cancer, my family pretty much blowing apart, and me drifting off into drugs, apathy, and a lackluster, underperforming pre-med student experience at Muhlenberg College.

Free Fall

When I was 18, I climbed a 60-plus-foot cliff near Half Moon Bay in California. I had not planned to climb and was certainly not dressed for it (I wore Converse high tops and carried a camera). Just a kid doing what came next rather than having any kind of plan. Near the top I encountered soil that was just not climbable. I knew I was in trouble, hanging on the side of a cliff like Spiderman. I could not back down and could not go on up.

Suddenly, I lost my grip on the cliff. I remember the intense adrenaline rush and pushing off to turn around in midair as I fell. I don't remember anything else. I broke my ribs and my left ankle in three places and banged up half of my face. The rescue squad pulled me up in a basket. I should have died; I was doing 45 to 50 miles per hour when I hit the flat rocks at the bottom.

Later, while working at a tennis club in Lake Bluff, Illinois, I met a 19-year-old kid named Michael. He had no money, no career path, and no real future. But he had a wife and a child and was happy – at 19. Here's a young husband and father, flipping burgers for a living, and yet he had this peace and contentment. Somewhere he heard my *"falling off the cliff"* story. One day, he came up to me and said, "God has a plan for your life." I wasn't sure what that phrase meant. But I still look back on that moment as the first time I heard the call of God.

A few weeks after that, I kind of took God for a test drive. I asked Him to set me up with a girl who would love me as much as I would love her. Now, understand, I had never dated. Dating just to date never worked for me. Well, completely out of the blue, I met a girl and started to date. Didn't see that coming. It didn't last, but God accomplished His objective and got my attention. I was interested in this God!

So, when Michael invited me to his church, I went. It was a little 75-member Foursquare Church in Waukegan, Illinois. Nothing cool about it at all. At the end of the service, the pastor asked if anyone wanted to meet Jesus. I went there with no intention of doing or saying anything. But, at the pastor's question, my hand shot straight up like a rope had jerked it.

Something began to change in my life. Nothing sudden or dramatic; I continued to do drugs for about a year. I went to college. Much about my life appeared the same, but something had shifted in my heart. Something big. A purpose beyond me began to emerge. Something *out there* – a call – began to capture my thoughts and dreams. Another *Life* had, apparently, accepted my invitation to come into mine. I slowly began to live on higher ground.

In the years that followed, my altitude has continually increased. Because of the new heights of perspective, I see and understand more than I did at the lower elevations. That is not because I'm brilliant or strong; it is simply because God, in His everlasting mercy, invited me to "Come up here," where He lives.

Part 2

....

MESSAGES FROM THE MOUNTAINS

*The mountains and the hills
Shall break forth into singing before you,
And all the trees of the field shall clap their hands.*

– Isaiah 55:12

THE BIBLE SPEAKS OF THE EARTH MOURNING (JEREMIAH 12) and groaning (Romans 8). And, as we see in the referenced scripture, the Bible also says that mountains and hills will break forth into singing and that trees will clap their hands.

Because they were created by God, the various geological and life forms of the earth have voices. Perhaps they all hold ancient and mysterious messages for us. I and many others know that mountaineering pulls climbers into intimate communion and communication. We've all heard the messages from the mountains.

And, as John wrote in 1 John 1:3, what I have seen and heard I want to share with you. So, in the following pages, I will share from my heart about what I saw and heard in the high places.

CHAPTER 6

WHAT IS THE MOUNTAIN?

....

I BELIEVE YOUR MOUNTAIN IS THAT SPECIFIC CALL GOD HAS FOR your life. It is a unique and sacred place to you, the Everest for your life. And at 61, I am just now moving into the fulfillment of it.

The call of God is not necessarily to some role or position that might appear as the pinnacle of success. His call is not a path to a corner office, and maybe not even to Christian ministry. Maybe your call is to an unnamed peak.

You will have many hills and mountains to climb in your lifetime, but there is one that rises high above the rest way off in the distance. That mountain calls to you; it seems to say, "*Come on. Way out here. Climb high; breathe deeply. Push hard. Press on, and never give up. I'm waiting for you. What I have for you cannot be found on those lower peaks. Don't settle for less than this extraordinary summit.*"

I've always had that sense. Over my 35-year career, I've achieved some impact on people and business ventures, and I have attained what most would call success. But none of that was *the* call for me.

It was all preparation for His call. There was always the hunger for something, some things noble, some things crazy. Like you, I always wondered if those dreams would ever be fulfilled.

For most of us, that great mountain of our calling is not accessible by any major highway or even a well-traveled path. The mountain is often surrounded by raw, desolate wilderness.

Through the Smaller Peaks

Most mountains are surrounded by hills and smaller mountains. Climbing those smaller peaks is essential to getting to the base of *the* mountain and then to the summit. You will not be able to live or perform effectively at the higher levels unless you have learned the lessons from those training climbs.

Most people never get past life's smaller peaks. Of those who do, some never even reach *the* mountain. Very few ever stand on the summit. My prayer is that *you* will be among the climbers who stand on the summit of His Holy Hill. And not just once. I hope you will walk there daily.

To walk on the heights of the earth routinely is to walk in the fullness of God's glory, His abiding presence, and His unique plans for you over the course of a lifetime. It is to live fully for the cause of Christ. It involves climbing many mountains, each one representing a specific task or call that He has for you at that precise point in time. That call is most probably not a one-time event or some task that has an end point. It is more likely a call to a lifetime role. Getting to the top of any mountain, natural or spiritual, requires training, focus, determination, endurance, sacrifice, a solid support team, and hard work. And, just as in natural mountaineering, higher altitude spiritual climbing can be very dangerous.

The View from Above

In Spiritual Mountaineering, you push above the low clouds of life and the spiritual air pollution that impair your vision. From above, you see your world from an entirely new perspective.

When I climbed Mount Rainier, we started out at 5,400' – in a cloud. With such low visibility, we could not see 500 feet above us. At about 9,000' we broke out above the clouds to behold an incredible view. Below us, a soft cloud deck obscured the hills, valleys, and lower peaks. Above us, the awesome mass of the high mountain soared to kiss the sky. That sky was a luminous blue that simply cannot be seen from down in the polluted lower atmosphere.

At lower altitudes, mountaineers see rivers to cross, hills and ridges to climb, and canyon walls — all barriers and hindrances. Furthermore, they can't see how all those landscape features fit together. So, finding the right path often entails a lot of guesswork, false starts, and backtracking. For most of the journey, a climber cannot even get a glimpse of the summit. Only when he or she reaches the high ground can they clearly see the layout of the landscape below—the hills, valleys, rivers, and roads. From high above, they lay out as clearly as a map.

So How Do I Get There?

Have you ever marveled at the great investment athletes, military personnel, public safety officers, teachers, and other heroes make? They exert themselves beyond the normal limits of human endurance. Many leave it all on the field, in the classroom, up the stairwell of the burning building, and on the battleground. Those who survive find an entrance to a rare fellowship with the few who have put everything on the line and spent every drop. No one else can stand in that circle of honor. Mountain climbers are like that too.

Why?

Mark Duggin recently talked to me about the curiosity of climbers. He asked, "What draws us climbers to explore the high and challenging terrains? Maybe what we call 'curiosity' is really the great mystery just hanging out there on the raw edge of the unknown. Do we keep risking injury and life because of some 'kingdom imperative?' Are we responding to the Lord's invitation to go on, to go further and deeper and higher? Is that what this is about?"

I saw he was right.

"Yes, I think so, Mark. That invitation and our response has been with us—at least me—throughout our, *my*, whole life! When we leave the safe, the familiar, we first encounter a sense of loss; we're leaving something. But, in reality, God is saying, 'No, I'm calling you *toward*...something!' So, we can't develop our curiosity about what He has for us—that new place, thing, event, relationship, this higher ground—unless we pay a huge price for it. It's like Jesus' story of the pearl of great price in Matthew. No matter what pearls the merchant already owned, he had to sell them to buy *that one*!"

Mark jumped back in, "Proverbs 25:2 says it's the glory of God to conceal, but the glory of kings to search out. And, The Message says, 'God delights in concealing things; scientists delight in discovering things.'[5] So, God keeps concealing and those caught in the grip of the mystery keep searching."

---

5 Verse taken from the THE MESSAGE: THE BIBLE IN CONTEMPORARY ENGLISH (TM): Scripture taken from THE MESSAGE: THE BIBLE IN CONTEMPORARY ENGLISH, copyright©1993, 1994, 1995, 1996, 2000, 2001, 2002. Used by permission of NavPress Publishing Group

If that's true, if we're all "caught in the grip of the mystery," why is it so gut-grinding to get to the top? Why do so few reach the summit? In my experience, I've seen four main obstacles:

1. **Lack of Vision:** We cannot achieve what we cannot see. Many read books or see movies about those who climbed mountains. But reading about someone else's experience is not enough. Only those who have vision burned into his or her heart will make the summit.
2. **Resistance:** Something seems built into the creation that makes us fight for every yard gained. Mountaineering is like other human struggles; it never comes easy. That's why many turn back. It takes a special quality of tenacity to claw your way up the side of a mountain.
3. **Discipline:** Military, law enforcement, construction, medical, mountain climbers, and other professionals know that discipline saves lives. In the crucible of a crisis, simple orders require simple obedience. Failure to follow orders can result in serious injuries or death. Our culture doesn't seem to understand the value of discipline or the consequences of mediocrity.
4. **Lack of Knowledge:** Mountaineering requires much more than physical strength and endurance. Climbers have to train for physical strength and endurance, master climbing and survival skills, and absorb great volumes of information about the mechanics of climbing, physiology, nutrition, weather, collaboration, arresting falls, etc. The failure to know can easily and quickly become the failure to survive.

My purpose in this book is to inspire you to find your vision, press on through challenges, have the discipline to stay with it long enough to get there, and equip you with the skills and knowledge you need to climb your mountain. Don't assume you already know enough. Even if you've learned a vast range of skills, procedures, and principles, read them again in the context and viewpoint of this book. It could turn on new lights of understanding. Furthermore, repetitions and redundancies on basic skills have saved many lives at high altitude. So, dig deep, examine every line for new insight and understanding in your preparation for ascending your mountain.

Remember that lower altitudes allow more room for learning and for error; the implications of mistakes are not as great or the fall as disastrous as when they occur at high altitude. The risks or implications at lower altitudes mimic what climbers see regularly at higher elevations. Up there, critical situations can arise in a split second. You have no time to sit down and study what to do. In the words of the Nike commercial: "Just Do It."

As climbers Mark Duggin and Brad Davidson learned (story in Chapter 3), weather is more volatile than we think. They were as prepared and equipped as mountaineers should be. But, when a blizzard roared up from the nearby Pacific coast, creating high wind and whiteout conditions, they had no time to Google the options or consult with others. They had to operate fast and in accordance with their training.

We must all confront the lie that we are not supposed to be extraordinary. Our view of meekness and humility has been twisted, making us think they mean being passive, acquiescent, and insignificant. But that defies our Creator's great purpose and plans for us, the works of His hands! The summit of God's Holy Hill is the fulfillment of His unique call for each of us.

My primary point here is life will deliver peak moments for us without warning. That's why we need to be ready to instantly release the extraordinary treasure God placed within each of us. In extreme situations or in routine life, the call is the same. Will you persevere as a mountaineer over the years that it takes for God to make the "Everest" of your life clear to you? Will you allow Him to lead you to its summit?

CHAPTER 7

TRAINING AND PREPARATION

....

Serious mountaineers train continuously, often for months, to prepare for major climbs. They often spend more time training than climbing. Climbers work on physical strength, cardiovascular capacity, balance, coordination, mental toughness, and endurance. They spend years training on techniques and equipment so that they can use them proficiently without a conscious thought. They train on lower, easier summits, refining and applying what they've learned where the risks and dangers are less acute. You don't climb above 25,000 feet without solid high-altitude experience. High altitude climbers are some of the most fit people on the planet.

Beyond extraordinary fitness, the most successful high-altitude climbers must objectively read their own performance in all situations; at low altitude or up high on an exposed ridge where the tolerance for error is razor thin. Russian climber Anatoli Boukreev, one of the best high-altitude climbers in history, studied his performance at high altitude for years. He could gauge his physical and mental performance, his nutrition and water intake needs, etc. so that when the stakes were high, he could quickly determine whether he should push further, stop and rest, or turn and head back down to the lower camp.

A climber must have the mental toughness to deal with things that would make most people run for cover or go weak at the knees. They can confront life and death decisions while maintaining the proper balance between objectivity and personal concern for themselves and their teammates.

Inexperience contributes to many mountaineering disasters. That is also true for Spiritual Mountaineering. It may set you up for poor judgment or simple mistakes at crunch time. Both can have disastrous results for you or your team, and you may never climb again. How prepared are you for Spiritual Mountaineering, where the conditions may be harsh, the air thin, the slopes steep, and the work harder than anything you have ever done?

If you have not adequately prepared yourself, you will never make it above the lowlands. You must invest time and effort in your basic training. If you do not regularly focus on the basics, you won't have what it takes when you are breaking a new trail, high on an exposed ridge in a fierce storm. Basic Training is not very exciting, but it gives you the foundation for living fully in God's call.

Are We Serious About Mountaineering?

Before we could start the climb on Mount Rainier, we had to go through a full day of training on key basic tools and techniques for mountaineering. We were taught how to stop a fall using a variety of methods. Over and over, we slid down the snowfield slope on our backs, on our fronts, head first, feet first, whatever. The guides had to *know* that we could stop a fall immediately. We went through similar repetitive training to demonstrate proficiency as part of a rope team, with a range of climbing steps designed to conserve energy and strength over a long haul. If we did not make the grade, we were not allowed to climb. And that was short, focused training to give us the bare minimum skills and knowledge necessary to make a very closely guided climb. Obviously, the preparation for a high-altitude climb (like Mount Everest or even Mount McKinley) would be much longer and more rigorous.

Spiritual Mountaineering is even more demanding. I often wonder: *Are we serious as Christians*? Why are we unwilling to prepare and train for this extraordinarily great adventure? Why do we not invest the kind of discipline that mountain climbers accept as normal and essential preparation?

If you have never really pushed yourself to the summit, you may have settled for an existence that is comfortable, convenient, and gives just enough return on investment to make you feel you're doing the right thing. But that approach may prevent you from clearly seeing life's possibilities. There is no greater tragedy than looking back at one's life and realizing you never really lived.

Clearly, Christians could benefit from a mountaineering approach. God deals with us much like our trainers on Rainier. If you haven't effectively trained, God may not allow you to ascend the mountain. In His mercy, He may keep us from the higher altitudes where just a mis-step or failure could be catastrophic.

Jesus trained; He pushed Himself. He climbed to the heights of crucifixion on Calvary; He paid the price. God led Him to a place that is higher than any human had ever been. In going there, He broke the trail that Spiritual Mountaineers can follow.

Four Stages of Learning

Regardless of what we learn, all of us progress through these four stages in one manner or another. Abraham Maslow's *"Four Stages for Learning Any New Skill"* certainly applies to our walk with God.

- Unconsciously incompetent
- Consciously incompetent
- Consciously competent
- Unconsciously competent

In some respects, the first stage is blissful ignorance; *I don't know what I don't know and I really don't care.* I am not aware that I am totally incompetent at a skill.

The second stage is extremely frustrating, but it is also the dawn of insight. I am now aware that I am incompetent at this thing; but, unfortunately, I keep repeating the same poor performance.

The third stage is real change! At last, I have figured out how to do what is required, but it takes some serious concentration to perform well each time. But that is progress!

The last phase is success. I have pushed myself to learn what it takes to truly master this thing; that's when it becomes my nature to hit the mark. Most top-flight athletes say they have to train to the point where performance just happens naturally.

True, effortless competence at anything comes through endless practice. Over and over, day to day, and year to year, we focus on the basics, pushing ourselves to learn more, become stronger, increase our capacity, press our endurance a bit further, and stretch further than we thought we could. Basic training is not fun or exciting, but it builds habits and deep reserves that keep us in the fight when others bail out.

We see that pattern so vividly in the lifestyle of the mountaineer. Because the dangers are so great, wise climbers (also known as "survivors") study diligently and train intensely. Shouldn't those who follow God emulate that same pattern of rigorous preparation for life on the mountain of the Lord? As I've lived more consistently and profoundly on the mountaintop over the last three years, the fruit of a passionate 40-year pursuit of God and training in the principles of a spiritual life have become so very clear. I have discovered the value (and thrill) of a consistent prayer and devotional life, patterns of searching the scriptures, and learning from experienced and wise "climbing guides." Fundamentally, it's all about staying connected to the Holy Spirit, hearing His voice, and responding. The inertia that comes from these daily disciplines will equip us for the dull routines, as well as the thrills, and the dangers we face in walking with the Lord.

What is Real Strength?

Training and preparation are designed to produce real strength. But what is that?

A plaque hangs in our house: "There is nothing so strong as gentleness, there is nothing so gentle as real strength." Real strength does not need to make a display of itself in order to authenticate itself.

Strength is a gift, but we increase that strength by working out, by heavy lifting. We all need resistance training. Do you realize that *nothing* comes your way without God's foreknowledge? If we stand firm and resist the storm or temptation and surrender to Him, everything that comes our way can make us stronger. That includes those life experiences that are confusing or feel like a Category 5 hurricane. Part of real strength comes from knowing that the Lord always leads us in His triumph (2 Corinthians 2:14), even when it may look like disaster. For me that hurricane struck when I was diagnosed with Parkinson's. But as I moved past the initial shock and "leaned into God," it became abundantly clear that God had a plan to use it in an incredible way.

As each of our kids went through middle school, they passed through the typical life-developmental stages regarding tough homework or difficult subjects. Initially, they tended to cave in and give up when they ran into anything difficult or confusing. As I pushed them to dig deep, they eventually started to figure out how to solve problems on their own, with only little outside help. In one evening of particularly difficult "coaching," I blurted out, "None of the problems in the textbook are intended to be unsolvable. Every one of them has an answer, and the authors wrote each, knowing that you can find the answer if you dig hard and deep enough."

The Eternal Purpose of Training

In his book, *Destined for the Throne,* Paul Billheimer wrote that Christians are being trained to resist all of the powers of this earth. In other words, all of life's trials are intended to make us stronger and equip us for our ultimate calling. To paraphrase Billheimer, "Asking God to remove the trials and challenges in life is like the hurdler asking the coach to remove the hurdles during track practice." You won't be much of a hurdler if you always get your way.

Sometimes the training involves short duration, heavy lifting. Sometimes it's a long-distance endurance run. Endurance training is sometimes the most difficult for me. Long hours on a bike (or running mile after mile). Boredom, the need to push on and on, my lungs screaming for a break, dry mouth, muscles like rubber, and my joints hurt. Who wants to sign up for that?

In addition to spending hours on a StairMaster, my training for Rainier included carrying 50 pounds of cat litter in a backpack while I hiked up and down the longest and steepest hill I could find in Austin, Texas. And it was in the heat of the summer when it was around 100 degrees every day. Back and forth, up and down, as long as I could take it. I pushed myself to the edge of dizziness. I knew that pushing hard then (when a fall would mean maybe a scraped knee) would keep me strong and focused when I was at 14,000 feet with the wind blowing 40 mph and the wind chill dropping toward zero. Mark Duggin learned that hours of laps up and down stadium steps can be a climber's best friend.

God puts us through strength, resistance, and endurance training to prepare us for the climbs in life. Sometimes, He throws us into brute force heavy lifting in order to resist the attack of the enemy. He may call us to intense prayer over our children, to cover them against the assaults of the storm. Sometimes, God sends us into spiritual warfare, to break the hold of sin's legacies that have tormented a family for generations. It could be a long run out in the desert to stretch personal endurance. Keep on, breathe deep, suck it up, push on, pound it out; mile after mile. No matter what the circumstance, He desires that we fulfill Hebrews 12: 1, 2: "Therefore, since we have so great a cloud of witnesses surrounding us, let us also lay aside every encumbrance, and the sin which so easily entangles us, and let us run with endurance the race that is before us, fixing our eyes upon Jesus, the author and perfecter of faith, who, for the joy set before Him, endured the cross, despising the shame, and has sat down at the right hand of the throne of God."

Many of us have heard that God won't allow us to face battles we aren't prepared for. And, yes, He does train us for battle. But, it is also true that sometimes we just have to go into battle, scared to death, and so weak. That's because, according to Hebrews 11:34, sometimes our weakness gets turned to strength. We become strong *in* battle. Those people can "put whole armies to flight."

Another aspect of training is learning the limits of your performance capabilities and then gradually pushing beyond those limits to max out your capacity. Most of us can endure more than we think we can. I want to push my capabilities to the limit on all fronts: physical, mental, and spiritual. Why? Because I want to present a vessel that is as fully capable as God intended me to be. I want to max out the design specs. But how do you do that?

A coach who works with top-flight professional athletes wrote about how he taught race car drivers to continually probe and extend the limits of their performance. For him, the key is learning what the edge looks and feels like and how you perform there. Knowing that, you then thoughtfully identify when and where it is right to push slightly beyond the edge. His insights certainly apply beyond athletics:

Whether you are a gymnast about to try a move never done before in competition, a runner trying to lower another record, or a driver about to roll out for a session, you most probably have a preconceived notion about what can be accomplished. What you think is the maximum can limit your performance.

Find and explore the maximum. By incorporating maximum effort and steadily pushing against and breaking through your comfort zone, you will develop and establish new skill levels which will not only bring you more speed, but will also force you to invent and strengthen your coping skills for catching and correcting mistakes. Additionally, this will lead to more confidence in your abilities. Keep lightly pushing against those barriers and they will move back. But we need to be very intentional about which situations are appropriate for the risk/reward nature of pushing our capabilities.

But I need to stress that your approach should be incremental enough where a mistake is a correction and a loss of speed, not a spin or an off.[6]

Mistakes will happen, every lap. By pushing in a way that you know what you are changing and you can proactively mitigate the implications of failure, the mistakes will be small and can be corrected as they happen. Analyze, understand, and put them behind you by the next corner, not to be repeated again. There is no perfect lap, so do not let a mistake set you back mentally for the rest of that lap or longer. I have seen plenty of pole laps with a "big" mistake in them.

Working on pushing your comfort level will not only find you more speed and develop your coping/recovery skills but will make you better on race day or at high altitude when it all really counts. Do not let others or your own mind limit what you can achieve.[7]

Most of life is practice. Very often it is a train-and-wait exercise. History, including the biblical record) is full of stories of men and women who were called and prepared. But then they had to wait—sometimes many years—for the fruition of their life purpose. Noah, Abraham, Sarah, Joseph, Ruth, David, and Paul are great examples.

Too often, Christians seem to run on into action without the disciplines of life worked into their constitution. Brute force training pays off when you have been in the desert for months without real refreshment, can't remember the last time you saw the flowing river of life, or when you are pinned down on an exposed ridge by high

---

6 Refers to sliding off the track.
7 Mike Zimicki, *Speed Secrets: Approaching and Surpassing Your Limits*.
   Winding Road, Dec 1 2014. https://www.windingroad.com/articles/blogs/speed-secrets-approaching-and-surpassing-your-limit/

winds. Resistance training will supply the depth and strength to gut it out.

The Heart of a Steward

In Phil 4: 11-13, Paul wrote that he had learned to be content in all things. In Romans 8:37, he wrote, "we overwhelmingly conquer." That is the same man who was shipwrecked, stoned, imprisoned, and left for dead. How did he do that? He *learned* a whole new way of life. He learned God's great love for him. That gave him contentment, regardless of the circumstance. Further, as a bondservant, he had no:

- Ownership of anything, including his life
- Agenda of his own
- Rights

Think of it; there was no way anyone or anything could disappoint, frustrate, insult, offend, or anger him. As a bondservant, he only walked in God's agenda. Do you think we can live like that?

CHAPTER 8

WHAT'S IN YOUR PACK?

....

*I*F YOU'VE EVER GONE WILDERNESS CAMPING, YOU KNOW THAT all of the things you carry in your pack can be broken down into a few simple categories: food/sustenance, clothing, safety/survival, first aid, orienteering, transportation, and shelter. The basic stuff for life all conveniently and efficiently jammed in your pack.

The stakes are much higher for mountain climbing. What you carry for mountaineering can mean the difference between a peak experience and disaster. A missing item could mean you don't survive. On the other hand, overburdening your pack could also be a significant, or even deadly, hindrance.

You must bring *everything* that could be critical to the mission – both for an ordinary climb or one that encounters serious difficulty. Everything you carry must have the optimal combination of weight, function, and size. You don't carry large or heavy things if you plan to make the long haul up the mountain. You have to plan carefully to be sure you have what you need and don't have anything you don't need. Nothing missing. Nothing extra. Stay lean and aerodynamic, no loose ends out flapping in the wind.

The challenge to mountain climbers is very serious: Planning must anticipate *whatever* may arise. No story captures that dimension any better than Mark Duggin's and Brad Davidson's climb. A simple shovel saved their lives (many climbers don't even carry shovels). I asked Mark to describe the crucial role of packing:

Packing Light and Right

Alpine adventures start with star-filled skies that give way to majestic sunrises and bluebird skies. Those sights are some of the timeless reasons to even go into the mountains. But, these experiences are far from guaranteed. When equipment breaks, a climber falls or is injured, the weather turns fierce, or any other crises appear, the contents of your pack can literally mean the difference between life and death. Some items may seem cumbersome—until they save your life!

On our 2016 Rainier climb, the contents of our packs preserved our lives through the three days we were caught in the storm. Although we intended the summit push to only take part of the day, we carried gear to spend the night if required. Turns out, that's exactly what we faced. Not only did we have the necessary gear, but creativity with that gear saved our lives.

For example, had we not taken shovels with us, I don't think we could have survived. Once we found our packs after summiting, we clearly saw we would not be descending, not with near-zero visibility and a blizzard trying to blow us off the mountain. We quickly chose the best spot for a snow cave and started digging. Because we were close to the summit, with constant freeze/thaw cycles, we had to hack through ice for over seven hours, just to create a space large enough for the two of us.

I have often referred to that space as an ice-casket, not because I thought we would die there, but the space was that small; it was like lying in a casket with the lid shut. But, it saved our lives. Besides the shovels, food, water, extra gloves, first aid kit, etc., we also carried a few other items that turned out to be crucial to the construction of the snow cave—trekking poles, a bivy sack, and an avalanche probe.

The trekking poles were not an item one would necessarily have on the summit of a glaciated mountain, but we grabbed them almost haphazardly as we started the summit push.

We ended up with a horizontal shaft tunneled into the mountain with a roof made of a bivy sack (thin nylon cover in the shape of a sleeping bag). A truss system, consisting of four trekking poles and two avalanche probes, supported the bivy sack roof. And, we used the shovels, ice axes, ice screws, and crampons to stake the roof down. Even with that structural support, we had to keep clearing the falling snow so the roof wouldn't collapse and trap us inside.

The items in our pack, mixed with improvisation and intentionality, kept us alive over the three days. That's the critical value of proper packing.

Finding that sweet spot of how much gear to take, physical training to endure, and skills to update/practice may not be immediately obvious, but intimately affect the process of the journey and the outcome.

Exchanging Your Pack for His

The same goes for climbing the Mountain of God. You need the necessities, but you don't carry extra baggage to the summit. You will never make it to the summit if you drag stuff around. You and I know what that stuff is. It includes the junk from our past that keeps us from finding freedom. Paul had a shameful past; if anyone had justification for being held back by his past, Paul did. Are your still carrying spiritual baggage, chains, and weights in your backpack? How long do you want to keep carrying that garbage around? Another couple of days, another month, or will five more years do it? At some point, climbers need to resolve somewhere deep inside that you are done with it; it was real; but you are done with it.

Maybe Jesus really meant it when He said, "Come unto me all who are weak, weary and heavy laden… Take my Yoke upon you for my burden is easy and my yoke is light." If so, maybe it would be wise to exchange your pack for His. Can we come to Him, lay our own pack of stuff down and refuse to pick it back up again? Could we let Him give us a brand-new pack? One that is easy and light?

Proper Diet

On the Rainier climb, just as the sky was beginning to lighten, I mentioned to my rope mate that I was getting a little hungry. Noah, our team guide, overheard me. We were at about 12,000′ and had a long way to go to the summit. At the next rest stop, while we were watching the sunrise paint the sky, I noticed Noah speaking with Alex, the lead guide. Then he walked over to me and said, "OK, Jim, you've burned through your deep energy reserves too quickly and you are now working off simple, quick energy foods. If you don't do something to replenish the deep reserves at this rest stop you will never make the summit. Do you have any foods that are primarily fats or proteins rather than carbs or sugars?"

I knew what he meant; carbs and sugars are great for quick energy bursts. Proteins and fats take longer for your body to digest and, therefore, are a lasting source of energy. You need a balance of both types of foods to have the kind of energy to make the long haul to the summit.

Because I was not an experienced climber, I had gone to a good outdoor supply store and stocked up on those "high tech" energy bars. You may have tasted some of those bars. Hard as oak and about as flavorful. Noah, like most of the guides, brought left over Pizza! Oh, and he brought one other quick food, one that he (after a detailed review of nutritional information) found to be the most complete and balanced supply of sugars, proteins, carbs, and fats in a small package—Snickers Bars! So much for high tech, scientifically formulated, expensive concoctions.

So, when he asked me about my food, I showed him what I had. He shook his head and, without saying a word, handed me a Snickers Bar. He usually brings some extras for clients, just in case. I'm guessing he's been through that on almost every climb. So, I polished off the Snickers and we moved on up the mountain.

Spiritual Mountaineering also requires a balanced spiritual diet with all major "food groups." In order for God to know He can call you into service in a snap, you must have consistently consumed a nutritionally balanced spiritual diet.

Are many Christians malnourished? We live in a very busy and information-saturated environment. The culture trains us to break everything into small bits. For example, we think we are communicating when we post a short burst on Facebook or Twitter. And we try to live on quick prayers while jogging, or a short page from a devotional book, and maybe daily readings of Psalms or Proverbs. How can we be healthy if we ignore the prophets, the gospels, and epistles? Yes, the "heavy stuff."

In simple truth, if we do not keep a balanced diet, we will lack the reserves to reach the summit in our walk with the Lord. The reason many never notice it is because they only travel in the lower elevations. They are never confronted with the implications of an imbalanced diet.

As in Hebrews 5:12-14 and 1 Corinthians 2:6, 3:1, and 12:20, mature Christians can handle solid food. The immature can only consume milk and other foods that can be chewed and swallowed easily. Solid spiritual food, meat, has to be chewed on, studied a while, and prayed about. Just like proteins and fats, the heavier parts of scripture are the slow- burning energy reserves that give you the enduring strength to make the summit.

Know Your Equipment

Every item in a climber's pack is critical. Each thing has a function and often serves multiple purposes. Climbers know how each piece works, and they know it well enough that they can find and use it in total darkness. Emergency situations demand quick action. No time to refresh your memory on how this thing works or how to tie a secure knot. You have to be "unconsciously competent" with every item.

We spent most of the first day on Rainier learning the equipment. We were taught how to climb with an ice axe so that we could respond to a fall quickly and safely. We learned how to use our boots and crampons to climb safely and efficiently, how to work on a rope team, how to configure our packs to fit comfortably, and how to set up our climbing helmet, climber's lamp, and climbing harness, etc. For those of us who knew nothing about climbing mountains, that was a lot to absorb in a short time. In a longer expedition seminar, the training covers much more of the full scope of mountaineering and can take up to six days.

Shouldn't those who plan to ascend the Hill of the Lord be just as serious and knowledgeable about their spiritual equipment? Because of the terrain, temperatures, and other conditions, a "minor mishap" could turn into disaster. That could be why the scriptures contain so many references to our spiritual equipment or weapons...belt of faithfulness, sword of the spirit, helmet of salvation, breastplate of faith, etc.

Packing for a long, hard climb up a mountain requires a critical review of everything in the pack. There are many things that a climber would love to take, things that would give more comfort or warm familiarity. Serious (and successful) climbers must be ruthlessly critical and honest about loading the pack *only* with that which is essential for the climb.

CHAPTER 9

WHO'S ON YOUR TEAM

....

No one climbs Mount Everest without support. Of course, some are thinking Reinhold Messner made a successful solo climb from Base Camp in 1980. That's true, but he had a support team at the Base Camp. Joe Simpson and Simon Yates got very close to a solo high altitude climb when they climbed a remote, little-known, 21,000-foot peak in Peru with no real support. They described the experience in "Touching the Void." They got as close to absolute disaster as one can get and still survive. It is virtually impossible to be successful on any high altitude bid alone. No one has ever done it; I doubt anyone ever will.

Why? Because no one person can plan, execute, and coordinate all of the things essential to a climb like that. No one person can maintain the required focus, objectivity, and judgment in the face of the brutal conditions that can arise quickly on a serious mountain. The summit of Everest is the only place on earth that pierces the jet stream; winds often reach 150 miles an hour up there. No solo climber can rescue himself or herself after a fall at that altitude and have any hope of making it back to safety.

The same is true on the Mountain of God. The Lord never intended for us to be solo climbers; He designed us to be interdependent; we need each other. In the early days of our marriage, I had to face losing my identity in marriage; what would happen *to me*. But, in my struggle, I learned that the real me could only become clear through my passionate commitment to God. Only when I found clarity in my identity as His son could I become a true partner and soul mate to Beth. My real identity isn't a stand-alone me, but a fully interdependent me. Knowing who I was in God gave me the base to lose myself in the marital relationship. That's when I could exchange what I thought was my identity for one that is inextricably bonded to Beth. That was precisely God's plan. Together, husbands and wives become far more than the sum of what either could have ever become on their own.

That's why we must have people in our lives who can challenge and correct us. The Bible clearly speaks to the need for unity and love between brothers and sisters. Unity brings power, effectiveness, and victory. Division and individualism bring disarray and defeat.

One of Satan's primary strategies is to isolate us from support and fellowship. Just as prolonged exposure to high altitude will impair perception and decision-making, prolonged exposure to harsh spiritual conditions can compromise spiritual acuity and weaken judgment. That can lead to life- threatening situations before we can even recognize the danger. For as long as we are compromised like that, we remain cut off from supply lines and the vital connection with the people and things that will keep us alive. Our common enemy will try to convince spiritual climbers that no one understands their unique situation, or cares, or will step up to help in a time of need. If he can keep them out there in that frozen wasteland, he has more opportunity to string together a sequence of events designed to take them out.

Base Camp

Establishing a Base Camp is one of the absolute prerequisites for any serious mountaineering attempt. Base Camp is the springboard of the expedition. It is the main supply depot, the communications and planning hub, the hospital, mess hall, the rest area, sanity checkpoint, etc. It is staffed by those closest to you, those you trust with your life. If a mountaineer has not assembled and developed a solid Base Camp, the expedition will probably fail.

In the very same way, the people in your immediate circle of Christian relationships will provide the Base Camp support for your ascent. They will be your prayer support and source of encouragement; they will admonish you, come alongside and care for you when you are injured, and launch a rescue if you go down. If I miss the mark with my spiritual Base Camp and neglect to build them up, equip and develop them, I won't be able to climb very high. I may make solo climbs above Base Camp, but I will never reach *the* summit.

An expedition leader purposefully combines a matrix of skills and experience when he or she selects the Base Camp team. Team members are carefully selected for their abilities and for how they complement the others in filling the roles critical to the success of the expedition. They select people for their raw determination, endurance, expertise in logistics, cooking and nutrition, medical care, load carrying, specific types of climbing (ice, rock, expedition or alpine style), etc.

In mountaineering, the actions of one can endanger the whole team. For that reason, each team member must have the courage to get in the face of anyone, in order to confront bad judgment or decisions, risky behavior, and to keep someone from walking into disastrous consequences. The people on the team will monitor how the climbers are doing, when they have been out too long at high altitude, and quickly and objectively measure if a climber is showing signs of exposure, hypothermia, pulmonary or cerebral edema, or anything else that might spell disaster. Base Camps schedule regular radio communication with each climber to make sure they keep their finger on the pulse of the climb itself and on each individual climber. That team is the foundation of the climb. The Base Camp team can actually make the call to pull back or scrub the climb altogether. They take that role very seriously; after all, they are the ones who will mount a rescue and risk their lives for a climber. They stay on the line to talk climbers through a long, cold, dark, and perhaps stormy night until the morning breaks. They can keep climbers from slipping off into the void and being lost forever.

A gap in any one of these things could mean delay, missing a window for the summit, or disaster because something or someone comes up short.

As a Spiritual Mountaineer, who's in your Base Camp?

First and foremost, your Base Camp is made up of your immediate family. No exceptions. Too many Christians neglect their primary Base Camp and are therefore at risk for disaster. It is important to pray for and with them regularly. Keep all of the relationships open, real, and vital. Furthermore, you should serve as part of *their* Base Camp. While they are essential to your climb, you may also be vital to theirs. If you neglect your responsibilities toward them, you are, very likely, setting them up for a fall.

I realized long ago that, like most people, I could do many things in my life, such as business success, ministry impact, or passionate pursuit of the recreation I enjoy. But if I miss the mark with my wife and kids, all the rest of it is worthless. Nothing is more important than family. I could influence thousands of lives and be recognized by many as a great leader, but if I do not fulfill my responsibility to be the godly head of my home and create an environment where they can flourish in Christ, I will have fallen short.

Next, your Base Camp is made up of those Christians who are closest to you, your spiritual family. Christians can never fully achieve who they were meant to be outside of regular and strong fellowship with a solid body of believers. As members of your Base Camp, they must know when you are doing well and when you need help. They must see it – often before you do. Of course, they should be strong and sensitive enough to confront you when and how you need it.

Spiritual Mountaineering requires "climbers" to purposefully build and maintain close relationships with people who have spiritual skill sets different from their own. They need to complement the climber's personality and skills. Rather than focusing on weaknesses or negatives, the entire group should recognize that the differences and weaknesses are there by design! We are designed for interdependence. God intended us to be knit together to create a foundation that allows each climber to summit The Mountain.

Rope Team

The Rainier guide service worked very hard to teach all of us how to climb in a rope team. As a team traverses up the steep slopes, they go through a seemingly endless series of switchbacks. Each turn requires the climbers to execute a very specifically choreographed sequence of movements. Climbers must keep the rope on their downhill side; otherwise it could slide under their feet. Loose rope and boots with crampons do not get along well in close company. Rope accidents can spell disaster before you have a chance to do something about it.

As climbers turn, they have to carefully step over the rope to move it to the downhill hand once they are past the switchback. At the same time, they have to transfer the ice axe to their uphill hand.

It isn't as easy as it sounds because you have an ice axe in one hand, the rope in the other, a narrow path in which to plant each step, and anywhere from 30 to 70 pounds on your back. Furthermore, you're sucking air, and you are climbing a slope that is at least as steep as stairs, but with no distinct steps, and it's really cold.

The last climber on the team must flip the rope out of the preceding climber's path to keep it from entangling his or her feet. This is particularly crucial because, in addition to having to concentrate on the list of things I mentioned above, the front climber can't see behind him or her and can't turn in order to check things out.

Halfway up the mountain during our climb, after I had flipped the rope out of my climbing partner's way many times, I found a different view of accountability. The typical view of Christian accountability says that I am going to meet with you once a week and ask you questions that may make you squirm. And the last question will be, "Have you just lied to me in any of your answers?" The thought is that if a person knows he or she will face tough questions that will keep them from doing something stupid, they will be more open and honest. But that kind of negative motivation usually does not work for most people. The fear of punishment just is not a good motivator for many (including me). It has limited effectiveness and is retrospective.

The way climbers travel on a rope team is a much better approach to accountability. Instead of waiting for my brother to fall, it is better to be proactive. It's better and easier to prevent disaster than to clean up after. To do that I must maintain a close enough relationship to know his path, the timing of his "stride," when he is (and is not) moving well and be observant enough to actually see the hazard and recognize when he is at risk. As with the rope team, if I do it correctly, many times he won't even realize that I have kept him from a fall. Sometimes that means speaking the truth in love, sometimes just praying; sometimes I will take care of things without him even being aware of it.

For a rope team to function effectively, every member must understand and be committed to that level of interdependence with their teammates. I want to climb with spiritually mature people who recognize danger and take steps to prevent disaster before it happens! You are, in fact, your sister's keeper; you need to be the kind of teammate that does what it takes to keep her on the mountain. It is truly "I've got your back."

A Nigerian friend of mine gave me a beautiful example of this kind of mutual commitment. When someone in his home church moves or has some major project, the other members will show up to help. They would be offended if they were not allowed to help. We in America tend to make verbal commitments with no follow through. "I heard you are moving. Let me know when and I'll be there." "Sure, no problem." Then when that person gives the specifics on date and time, they too often hear, "Oh I'm so sorry, I have to take my kid to a soccer tournament." Or, "I am so busy with my job that I just have no free time." The uncomfortable truth is that we all have enough free time to work out, play golf or other things we enjoy. Time management is simply the way we set our priorities.

Speaking the truth in love, Nigerian style, works like this. If I demonstrate true commitment to a brother, that says, "I will inconvenience myself to help him whenever he needs it and I will not take no for an answer when I ask if he needs help." Then if I need to correct, or if God uses me to prune, refine, or sharpen him, he will trust and receive what I say. I've taken the time to build the relationship. The load of truth we deliver to our brothers and sisters can never exceed the strength of the relational bridge we have built. Only when I've built that foundation of love can I speak the truth in love more directly and have it hit the mark. Too many try to correct when they have not taken the time to build a weight-bearing relationship. But, if I do build a solid structure with him, then I have the basis for fulfilling Gal 6:1 & 2. Only then can I go to a brother in sin (or at risk) and bear his burden. Like a Base Camp member, I've earned the right to get in his face, or even to slap him around, to keep him from disaster.

One of the other critical roles the rope team fills is disaster response. We were drilled by the Rainier guide service on how to stop a fall. Get in the arrest position and stick to the mountain. Dig hard, kick in with everything you've got so that when the rope goes taut, within a couple of seconds after your teammate falls, you will hold them. One of the most profound lessons God taught me on Rainier was that I am my brother's keeper; if they fall, I will fight with everything I have to save them from going down. I will kick, and dig with my hands until they are bloody, to keep my brother or sister from disappearing into the void. I will do whatever it takes to keep them from falling, but if disaster strikes, I'll fight with every fiber of my being to keep them on the mountain.

Unity in Diversity

Selecting your teammates for Base Camp and your climbing team is one of the most critical success factors in your quest to climb God's mountain. Who you hang with does more to influence your future than most of us are aware. They need to have the same vision of, and commitment to, the summit. Further, they need to climb at roughly the same pace as you so the team is not continually fighting the length of rope between climbers.

The importance of this is most critically revealed when you are out on the ragged edge. Beyond blending a mix of skills, the most important factor in building a team is: Can they work together as a highly functioning unit? Does the group chemistry work? Can they work through problems and relational difficulties effectively? Do we all understand that our differences are designed to complement one another?

Sometimes churches tend to think that unity means uniformity; everyone must agree on all points. Naturally, a body of believers should have agreement on "the majors" of theology and ministry objectives and be mutually committed to one another. But it does not mean we are to be identical and agree on everything. The Lord's designed diversity in His Body is essential.

For example, Beth and I are very different people in many ways. I doubt any dating service would ever have put us together. But God did. One day, I grumbled to Him about some of our significant differences, like athletic and academic interests (all the stuff that I'm naturally inclined to like). Then, I heard God simply ask, "Why are you looking for apples on a peach tree?" No explanation was given or needed. It was clear; Beth has skills, interests, and characteristics that I don't have. God did that deliberately. He purposefully puts people together (in marriage and in other relationships) who have carefully designed differences. Together, we see, hear, feel, know, and do far more than either person could ever have done individually. If we were identical, we would not bring anything new to the relationship. God intends us to be different, to celebrate that difference, and be vitally interdependent.

Too many people have been trapped into focusing on the negative aspects of their interpersonal differences (complaining, failure, unmet and unrealistic expectations, etc.) with others. Too many marriages end in divorce because the man and woman didn't get God's plan for marriage and for them. If it weren't so tragic, it would be comical because God's response would be something like, "Yep, of course you are different people. That is exactly what I had in mind. The two of you, together, were designed to be much more than either of you could ever be alone."

The same principles hold true for your Base Camp and climbing team. You need to work to maintain a solid Base Camp and climbing team. And it takes work. You need to purposefully develop relationships with people of different background and experience. Together, you can build a Base Camp that includes the full complement of skills, characters, spiritual gifts, etc. so that each of you can reach the summit. Rather than disdaining the differences, run to them, celebrate them, and draw strength from them. Lean on them. To make the differences work you must have regular prayer and fellowship with them. It cannot be a distant relationship. Everyone needs to be absolutely committed to one another.

> "Be sure you choose those closest to you carefully, because 2000 feet up the side of a cliff is a bad place to have a discussion with your partner about how this whole 'rope thing' makes them feel tied down in the relationship."
> JOSHUA HARRIS

Losing a Teammate

On the 1982 attempt on the unclimbed North Wall of Everest, at about 26,000´, just below Camp 6, Marty Hoey, one of the most experienced women climbers in the world, leaned back to let climbing partner, Jim Wickwire, pass. As he climbed past her, Jim heard some carabiners rattling and the odd sound of a strap pulling past metal. He turned, only to see Marty disappear down the face. She was gone. Her climbing harness had unraveled. Because of a simple mistake with tying and double checking her harness, she fell 6,000´ to the base of the mountain. They never found her body. Naturally, it devastated the entire team. She was well liked and very highly regarded, as a person and a climber. That loss was one of the major factors that led to scrubbing the expedition.

Near the beginning of their descent from the summit of a peak in a remote region of the Andes, disaster hit Joe Simpson and Simon Yates. Just below 20,000´, Joe fell down a 10-foot drop-off and shattered his leg. Since they had to descend a very steep 4000´ wall of ice and snow, it meant Joe was a dead man. No one can save another climber in that predicament.

Or can they? Without a word the two men started working with extraordinary teamwork to lower Joe down the face on a rope. They leapfrogged their way to the bottom of the face, where it seemed to level off to the glacier at the bottom of the mountain. From there they could certainly make it the remaining six miles back to Base Camp and safety. Darkness fell as they worked their way down. Then, on the last "leap," Joe dropped off the edge of an ice cliff in total darkness and was left hanging in midair (they had no way to know how far he was above the bottom of the cliff). With his shattered ankle, he was unable to climb back up the rope. Simon was in a good anchor position, but because he had to maintain the position, he could do nothing to secure the rope and get down to a point where he could save his friend. For hours, he struggled to hold his anchor position.

Somewhere in the blank space of the dark overnight hours Simon felt his foot slip. Then he slipped further, and then a bit more. He slammed up against the most difficult decision a person could face. He would have to cut his partner loose, or neither of them would survive. Could you cut the rope to save yourself knowing that your partner would fall to a certain death? How would you face his parents when you come back alive and their son is left at the bottom of some crevasse more than 8000 miles away?[8]

Losing a teammate is absolutely devastating. It may mean the end of your climb. Of course, I'm talking about a geological mountain climb. But, what about losing a teammate in Spiritual Mountaineering? Why did Marty make such a simple mistake that cost her life? Why did Simon have to cut the rope to survive? Why did – fill in the name – perish and you survive? We don't know.

What if that teammate were your parent, spouse, mentor, one of your children, or your closest friend? The things that drew you to them—the wise counsel and spiritual insight, the strong grip to pull you up from a fall and secure you again—are gone in the blink of an eye. Since we're talking about fulfilling the call of God (and not a physical mountaineering experience), the next question is, can you continue? Will you will allow the loss of a teammate to keep you from finishing your race?

Will you get back on the mountain? God's plan for you still calls. The hurt, pain, fear, condemnation, guilt are real and profound. The fire you once had in your heart may be just a faint ember. But the call remains. You survived for a reason. No matter what the details of the situation or event, your survival was not an accident or random event. You can convert the loss and deep hurt into a source of strength and ministry. Maybe the one who passed away had indeed finished his course. Now he passed the baton to you. Is it possible that it is now time for you to pick it up and run your leg of the race?

---

8 In the conclusion of that story, Simon Yates did cut the rope, dropping his friend into a pitch-dark free fall of at least 70 feet. Simpson assumed he was a dead man. But, after crashing through ice formations which slowed his fall, he landed on solid ground. Alive. Despite his broken leg, he crawled eight miles back to their base camp. Today, he is a motivational speaker.

Summary

Who's on your team? Do they have what it takes to support you when you need it, confront you when you must see things more objectively, and to rescue you when you go down? Are they close enough on a regular basis to know your stride and be able to recognize when you might falter? Are they truly committed to you and you to them? Have you intentionally sought out people who have different skills, characteristics, and spiritual gifts to provide balance around you?

You were never intended to be a solo climber. We are at our best only when we rely on, and function within, the interdependences that God intended for every one of us. In fact, God purposefully holds us back from some summits until we recognize our need to be part of an interdependent team. Perhaps you've seen (or heard about) the photo of a turtle sitting on top of a fence post. The message is that he didn't get there by himself. None of us reach any serious pinnacle by ourselves. We weren't designed for that.

CHAPTER 10

PLANNING YOUR ROUTE

....

A MOUNTAINEER DOES NOT REACH THE SUMMIT OF ANY PEAK without thorough, diligent route planning. In developing that plan, mountaineers start with a general sense of the route to the summit and then study the mountain as thoroughly as possible. They examine detailed topographic maps, climbing guides, notes from other climbers or previous climbs, weather patterns for the last 12 months, current weather conditions, and forecasts for the days around the climb dates. Which stretches of the route are most exposed or pose the greatest risks? Where are the best intermediate camps or stopping points?

When the team establishes Base Camp, they reassess the plans for the route based upon detailed study of the current conditions on the mountain, of what is now in clear view. The entire focus is to manage risks and maximize the likelihood of success before they even take the first step. Throughout the climb, the mountaineers will continually revisit and revise plans and options based on conditions.

They lean on the best of their abilities to plan the route that will give them the highest likelihood of making the summit.

The whole adventure comes down to *maximize likelihood of success, minimize risk, and prevent disaster.* That is only accomplished by thorough planning and exercising integrity at the moment of decision. That means subjecting plans to continual re-assessment, using the same principles and criteria as when we first developed the plans.

That is also how a Spiritual Mountaineer should approach climbing his or her mountain: integrate the best human planning, talent, and skill with spiritual sensitivity. Balance reliance on personal skills, experience, and abilities with God's creativity, field of view, and sovereignty.

Some think detailed plans will limit the Holy Spirit's freedom to lead. I don't believe that; in my experience, it is how we execute the plan that releases or hinders the Spirit. If we do a good job laying out plans, we will be better equipped to follow His redirection than if we had not planned at all.

Others do everything humanly possible to evaluate every contingency, do the full risk analysis, lay out a plan, and stick to it "come hell or high water" because God helps those who help themselves. In my view, both approaches are narrow and usually fail to lead to the mountaintop. I've found great wisdom in the maxims: "Failing to plan is planning to fail" and "If you never plan to accomplish anything in life, you will surely accomplish your objective." But it is not solely about planning and then blindly executing. How does it work? Does the answer only apply to long-range planning or detailed short- or immediate-term planning, or both? What does scripture show us?

The Bible includes great stories about planning. When God told Noah to build an ark, He gave detailed instructions about the materials and specs. Clearly, the size of that project (construction and gathering and boarding of the animals) required extensive planning and detailed execution. But it appears that God trusted Noah to use his own wisdom and talent to make the details happen. Genesis 6 does not indicate that God gave Noah precise details on how to build the ship—a large and complex task. Clearly, Noah did a lot of planning.

Nehemiah's construction project of rebuilding the walls of Jerusalem required an integration of planning and prayer. Similarly, In Genesis 41, God's direction and detailed planning by Joseph were both critical to feeding thousands of Egyptians for 14 years. It would have been impossible to maintain the food stores and fairly dispense them over that period of time without significant planning.

Finding the Route

Spiritual Mountaineers integrate the best of their abilities with the leading of the Holy Spirit; they live on a solid foundation of open communion with God. I've found prayer and knowledge of the Word to be essential. In that context, I draw on all my skills, experience, creativity, problem-solving abilities, and analytical skills to develop the plan that God is directing for me. Having settled on the immediate path, it's somewhat like the Nike commercial...Just Do It.

Like the mountaineer, we must constantly evaluate current conditions. That takes honest, objective analysis of what we see and hear so that we may clearly discern His voice regardless of the environmental noise. It also requires objective input from others I trust. Spiritual Mountaineers should always go – easily and naturally – to the reliable, mature believers in their Base Camp. After all, isn't that why you selected them as team members?

If I don't hear redirection, I execute the plan with everything I've got. But, if He tells me to do something different, I had better listen and follow.

Trust Your Guide

I know if I, as a Spiritual Mountaineer, get off course, God will redirect me to the path to the summit. *I trust Him.* The first moon launch was reportedly off-course 90% of the time. But, through course-correction, it hit its target. The astronauts trusted "Houston."

Sometimes, we all feel like we're groping in the dark, trying to find our way up the mountain. Despite all our best effort in planning and execution, sometimes, we just can't find the way. We have a hard time seeing the path beyond a few feet ahead, let alone the route above.

Why?

I think it comes down to this: I'm just a simple hand tool, carried around in God's tool bag until I'm needed. That's why I am often in the dark about where I am going. I'm just banging around inside the tool bag, ready to be used for my designed purpose. When it's time, God reaches into the bag to grab me. When He's finished with me, I go back into the bag and He leans back and says, "Look what I've done." And, that's as it should be; you wouldn't applaud the paint brush Leonardo da Vinci used to paint the Mona Lisa, would you? So, why do we promote and exalt the people God uses to do His work? You should also remember the paint brush must be clean and available when the Master needs it. If you've ever tried to paint with a dirty brush, you know exactly what I mean.

But God's route planning can be mysterious. Often, when God uses us, our "deployment" may be preceded by what appeared to be wasted time. Was God coordinating schedules to choreograph a divine appointment He set before the foundation of the earth? We realize later the appointment could only occur in a precise time window. As we went along, somewhat in the dark, He orchestrated events so that we met someone at the right time and place to be used by Him. In those times, we are like mountaineers, climbing in the dark, trusting that He knows the way. The morning light will reveal an awesome view where we will see our world from His perspective. The Lord knows the beginning and the end. He alone can be trusted with the past and the future.

Guides on how to manage your career path and maximize your potential fill many bookstore shelves. But, I've never found them to work. Every time I've read those books or reached out to recruiters, I've dug a dry well. Only when I surrendered to Him who sees beyond what I can see did I find a path far more suitable (and exciting) than the one the "professionals" could have planned. Trust Him with the uncertainties of life.

Summary

Ascending the Mountain of God pulls us into the greatest adventure possible. So, develop your plan, then trust and obey your Guide. Go out and "just do it" while looking and listening for His direction. Climbers never know what lies just around the next corner or above that next ridge. My long-range plans should always be somewhat fuzzy; I must trust my Guide for what lies beyond my field of view and scope of control. The plan is not the issue; it is what I do with the plan that determines what God will do through me.

CHAPTER 11

THE WAY OF THE MOUNTAINEER

....

*B*ECAUSE PEOPLE NATURALLY AND QUICKLY ACCLIMATE TO their environment, part of the challenge of mountaineering involves the sheer audacity of changing all that. We may live 40 years at 2800 feet, but then we dare to ascend to 14,000 feet. You can't do that casually. So, in this chapter, I want to give you a practical look at the way of the mountaineer, how they adapt to (and thrive at) high altitudes. After the training, planning, and great expense, how do we actually live at high altitudes?

Reaching the summit is a long and difficult process. It can be brutal. Even getting *to* the mountain often requires a long trek through the wilderness, a slow and frustrating grind. If a climber ascends too quickly, he or she can experience life threatening altitude sickness. Summit day is different from all others; it usually starts well before sunrise. Guides live by the maxim: "Reaching the summit is optional, returning to Base Camp to climb again another day is mandatory."

Expectations often bring frustrations and disappointments with mountaineering, and in life. If we had more realistic expectations, we would better handle the challenges. My first supervisory position required many manual assembly steps that preceded a very technical core manufacturing process. Almost every day, one or more production lines failed to start smoothly or quickly. That was frustrating to me and the people who ran the production lines. The start of our daily routine often looked like a three-ring circus. As the one primarily responsible for solving the technical problems, I spent nearly every morning running from one fire to the next. Just to get up and running

Naturally, that took a toll on all of us over the years. Then, I realized a key to minimizing the burnout rate would be to clearly explain that we should never expect a smooth operation. Adjust the expectations; help everyone understand that the workday would be unpredictable from the get-go. If we all could come in each day with realistic expectations, we would reduce the stress level. And, we saw it happen. People stayed in the fight over the long haul. If we understand our spiritual environment, and the process we are in, we will be much more able to handle it.

Expedition Style Mountaineering

Climbing big mountains (physical or spiritual) usually involves a long trek just to approach the mountain. The approach to remote peaks, including the major peaks of the world, can take weeks. During most of the approach and actual climb, you can often not even see the summit. Only as you keep climbing do you catch glimpses of it.

At the mountain, the team establishes Base Camp and then a series of other camps on their way to the summit. Each one is placed to be safe from avalanches and storms. Each camp is a pivotal stopping, resting, recharging, and launching point. Each one takes more to reach than the last one, but is the base for the next phase of the climb. Barring a mishap, as climbers progress up the mountain – through the series of camps – they become more acclimatized, accustomed to the heights, and prepared for summit day.

Consider how God takes people through different places and phases in life. Each one requires us to leverage previous experiences to press on to the next one. I see those roles as carefully designed to develop our skills. It all prepares us for that one climb that stands high above the rest. But, sometimes leaving one place that we love can be difficult; it sure feels like a loss. But God isn't asking us to leave a place as much as asking us to move toward something. By studying historic stories, such as those of Joseph, Moses, and David, we can see that God directed their development with high points and low valleys over long periods to prepare them for roles that changed the world. They learned the way of the mountaineer.

Joseph could have been (perhaps was) frustrated with the bizarre course of his life. Read the story in Genesis 37-47. Just when he seemed to be on the edge of a breakthrough, he was cut down. First, his brothers dumped him in a pit and sold him into slavery. Then, after being led by God to Potiphar, and after faithfully serving him, he suffered a great injustice and ended up in prison. No one would have faulted him for being frustrated with the bizarre course of his life. [9]

Do you see the same principles at work in your life? Maybe God has led you through a long sequence of career moves. They may seem like a logical progression; they may not. Perhaps He led you through difficult times. Maybe He gave you a year of rest (as He did for me). God's

---

9 I recommend Paul Billheimer's book *The Mystery of God's Providence* for a great meditation on that aspect of Spiritual Mountaineering.

timeline for reaching the summit is clearly not ours. It took me 60 years to get to Base Camp at the foot of my mountain. His ways are not ours, His definition of progress, success, accomplishment; impact, etc. are not limited by man's feeble definitions of the same. In his famous poem, "If," Rudyard Kipling called both triumph and disaster "imposters."

Acclimating to Altitude

During the early part of our Mount Rainier climb, we could look up at the summit through the clouds. It seemed so close, as though we might reach it quickly. But if climbers move up a mountain too quickly, they can develop altitude sickness. The symptoms— ranging from mild headaches to nausea to life-threatening pulmonary or cerebral edema—reveal the body's inability to deal with the lack of oxygen. At that point, respiratory or brain function can be seriously compromised (even to the point of death). The only real cure for altitude sickness is to move the climber back down to lower altitude – sometimes immediately.

1 Timothy 3:1-13 and 5:17-22 seem to speak of spiritual altitude sickness. That can happen when a new believer is prematurely elevated to positions of ministry or leadership. The very real dangers of that can range from minor mistakes to a fall that takes them out completely. The symptoms are very similar to natural altitude sickness: poor judgment, incoherent speech, loss of control, stumbling, and falling.

Sometimes, a leadership role in their professional life will make it seem natural to use (too quickly) those skills in a church. If that new believer is not grounded in the Word of God, basic disciplines of Christian life, and does not have a solid support team, elevating them too quickly can lead to disaster. Developing spiritual climbing skills takes time.

Breaking New Ground

In most high-altitude climbing, a team of climbers takes turns "pushing the route" or breaking the new trail. Being the first up a new route can be extremely taxing. That climber has to deal with whatever snow, rock, glacier, wind, and ice conditions are present with no secure physical support from above and sometimes little from below. The lead climber deliberately positions the rope that others use to climb safely. Proper placement minimizes the risk of certain ever-present hazards. Different climbers may be stronger in different types of climbing than others (for example vertical ice climbing vs. exposed rock or loose snow). The expedition leader determines who will lead each section of the route, based on the anticipated conditions.

As we climb, we should know that God may have others lead parts of the route for our climb. We should trust the skills within the team and trust our Guide to make the right assignments. If we do not rely on that teamwork, we may never get past that one section or have enough left in the tank to push on to the summit. We were never designed to be independent. God's plan has always been interdependence. In 1 Corinthians 3, Paul described the roles he, Apollos, and Cephas had in building the house of God in Corinth. Each one had a part in the overall work of the ministry. Esther understood it too. She knew she was raised up "for such a time as this" and that Mordecai had established some of the route before her.

Rest Stops

Eagles rest on the wind. They can reach great heights riding thermals without ever moving their wings. People cannot ascend in that way. But rest is still critical for humans. The press for the summit must be balanced with rest and recuperation so that a mountaineer has enough stamina remaining to finish the long hard climb, up *and* back down. If I rest too much at high altitude where my condition (just by being there) is deteriorating and my appetite is gone, I risk not being able to continue when the window for a summit bid is open. On the other hand, if I push too fast, I may drain my strength and have nothing left when the conditions are right.

That is why a Sabbath rhythm is crucial. Our bodies, minds, and spirits were not designed for continuous peak exertion. Trust the Guide when He says, "Stop and rest." Make the time and space to meet with Him. Dedicate as much time as it takes to connect with God, to linger there, truly converse, and rest in His presence. Jesus rose while it was still dark to get alone and refresh/reset with God (Mark 1:35). In Isaiah 58, the last requirement God gave before ministry was to observe the Sabbath.

In my 13-month period of rest in 2001 and 2002, the Lord provided income along the way; we never missed a payment. But, we didn't hear a peep from Him. The silence from heaven was deafening. But, as we came out of that desert, we realized it was all His plan. We needed the break from what had consumed me and to prepare for what followed.

In fact, it was one of the best periods of my life. He allowed me to be home more than ever before. I got to spend quality time with Beth and our daughters. He knew we needed it because we then entered a 10-month period of me working in one city with my family in another. We would not have survived—and thrived—had it not been for that year of rest.

When it's time for strenuous climbing, you need to hit it hard with focus and drive. But it's also crucial to develop a lifelong rhythm of rest so you have the long-haul endurance. A wise man told a friend of mine, "The issue is not how much work you can do in a day, but rather in a lifetime."

The Hillary Step

The most technically challenging section of the Southwest Ridge route on Everest is a 40-foot vertical wall of rock and ice at about 28,700′. Several had tried to climb it, but Sir Edmund Hillary was the first to get past it and make the summit in 1953. It is known as the Hillary Step.

The ridge approaching the step is a very narrow knife of rock, ice, and snow with very long – 8,000′ to 10,000′ – steep falls on either side. The face of the step runs at an odd angle to the axis of the ridge so getting on and off the step is difficult and dangerous. There are few handholds and footholds, and snow and ice cover the rock. Above the step, the ridge widens and eases to a relatively gentle slope up the last 300 feet to the top of the world.

In mountain climbing, the rate of ascent corresponds to the pitch of the slope or face, the altitude, the conditions of the surface (rock, snow, ice), the condition of the climber, and the weather. Sometimes progress comes quickly and easily. Other times, it is slow, painful, and dangerous.

Sometimes we move forward and upward at a very steady pace. Other times, we wonder if anything is happening at all. And, sometimes, a "Hillary Step" confronts us. Others tried and failed. But He brings us face-to-face with that vertical wall, perhaps to do what no one else has ever done.

During a difficult time for our family several years ago, I went for a long walk out in the woods. About a mile and a half back I sat down to talk with God. I shouted at the top of my lungs: *"What's Going On?"*

His answer was so direct and simple it was almost funny: "You are on a vertical face."

In those six words, He clarified everything. In three seconds, He changed my perspective. Because of His Voice, a difficult time was no longer a problem. I got up and went back home ready and able to deal with whatever came along. A different perspective can change everything.

Over the last few years, since reconnecting with Bob Hofmann and starting work on the pharmaceutical compound he developed, I've learned to recognize where God's grace leads us to move forward, often very quickly and efficiently. But, more importantly, I have learned to recognize where His grace is *notably absent*. More on that later.

We've all groped for handholds and footholds as we cling to a vertical wall high up on one of life's exposed ridges. Perhaps we haven't seen outward evidence of progress in a while and we wonder what in the world is going on. Maybe it's something we've tried to get past many times before. Or, it could be something no one has done before. It's not impossible; it's just that no one ever found the right approach. We often have to carefully, but with fierce determination, push past a vertical wall to see that the summit may be just a few feet beyond.

As Good as It Gets/Secondary Peaks

Around 5:30 am, at 12,000 feet on Rainier, sunrise transformed the view. I and the other climbers stood in awe as we watched from above the clouds. Only the largest peaks across southern Washington and northern Oregon rose that high. As God painted the sky with His own *new-every-morning* brilliant colors, we had an amazing view of the blown-out cone of Mount St. Helens, Mount Baker, and the pinnacles of Mount Hood and Mount Jefferson down in Oregon. Despite the critical need to keep my focus on my next step, I kept stealing glances at the changing majesty of the scene. The raw beauty and danger, the strain, challenge, and exhilaration made it one of the most memorable experiences of my life. To stand at the summit is to know why you were born. Our body wears down rapidly. But our spirit seeks the high altitude of God's call.

Roughly every two hours we stopped for a 15-minute rest. Each time we put on our down coats, sat on our packs, and tried to eat something and drink half a liter of water. The view from that "breakfast table" was like no other. At various points in climbing, thoughts cross your mind: *"Why do I need to go to the top? I have no idea what it will be like up there. The view from here is spectacular. It is probably not all that much better from up there. I think I'll just hang out here for a while and then head back down. This is good enough."*

In mountaineering, a climber may have to conquer secondary peaks on the route to the summit. For example, the South Summit on Everest is a smaller peak on the Southwest Ridge route. You can't get to the summit on that route without climbing over it. If you are not familiar with the route, or if cloud cover has obscured the real summit, you may conclude that you have reached your goal and are on the top of the world. But, in fact, you have more mountain to climb. What if every explorer or discoverer in history had that same attitude? America never would have been discovered and man would never have walked on the moon.

In writing this book, I do not want to stir up a restless spirit in otherwise stable Christians. On the other hand, though, we can never afford to let ourselves mistake stagnation for contentment. If we never dig deep in God to determine if there is something more, bigger, higher that He has prepared for us, we may never taste the incredible fruit of the Spiritual Mountaintop. Remember, we naturally reach for Him *up there*.

Summit Day

For most high-altitude climbing, "summit day" begins somewhere between midnight and 3 am. The main reason is that getting to the summit and back safely in daylight can take 20 hours or more. You need to start early so that you do not risk making the most dangerous parts of the descent in the dark. As the day wears on, the sun's heat can make the snow and ice soft and loose. When that happens, climbing conditions deteriorate, footing becomes less solid, and the risk for avalanches can increase dramatically.

On my Rainier climb we left the 10,000′ climbing hut at 1 am. As we climbed up through 12,000′, light began to soften the horizon. We had four rest stops of 15 minutes each and reached the summit at 9 am. After less than 30 minutes on top, we headed down and made it back to the 10,000′ hut in three and a half hours. While most of us had trained for a long time and were in the best shape of our lives, much of the climb above 12,000′ was just plain brute force. We climbed up a slope of ice and snow that was steeper than a stairway and had no steps. The wind was a steady 20 to 30 miles per hour, with gusts to more than 40. I was as tired as I've ever been, and I had a cramp in my gut that felt like a knife turning in my abdomen. *Pick up my left foot. Put it down in front of my right. Pick up my right. Put it down in front of my left. Take two forceful breaths. Pick up my left foot. Put it down in front of my right. Pick up my right…* for hours on end.

You just slug it out, pushing aside any hope of comfort. *Just stay in the game.* Of course, high-altitude climbing imposes more extreme examples of the brute force push to keep moving forward. That intense push can last 20 hours and more, all the while dealing with the knife edge between staying upright and slipping off into the void.

We have become so softened by our comfortable, American, Christian experience that most Christians don't have the constitution to deal with any serious challenge; they are, frankly, in no shape for the hard, determined push to the summit.

I wrote most of this book between 2 and 5 in the morning, over a four-year period that was one of the most challenging times of my life. When I started writing, I was the Senior VP of Operations for a Biotech startup. My role required me to deal with the challenges of launching an FDA- regulated product, building a facility, developing new products, defining strategic direction for the company's future, building a team, balancing that with gut-level day-to-day execution, etc. During my early years with the company, I worked between 60 and 80 hours a week. My travel schedule was difficult for our family. It took a very deliberate effort to carve out the time and energy for Beth and our four daughters.

Besides that, for the first year in that job I lived and worked in the Nashville area while my family was back in Austin, trying to sell the house during a real estate market crumble. The strain could have torn us apart. Because of a few simple, practical steps, and an unwavering determination to get through that, we grew stronger through it all.

My point in all of this is that, while my life may have seemed out of balance to some observers, that three- to four-year period was simply a very hard push with absolute dogged determination to press through. I had to remain focused; I would definitely make the summit on that climb, and make it down safely, with ALL of my family intact. I focused on making sure our family would become stronger in Christ. And it's only a season. It's not a lifestyle. Some seasons in life can be hard. But God is more than capable and ready to equip and assist us for the challenge and bring us back to Base Camp safely.

The Death Zone

In high-altitude mountaineering, the portion above about 25,000′ is known as the Death Zone. The oxygen level in that zone cannot sustain human life. The human body slips into an inexorable progression towards death. The loss of appetite becomes severe, the body does not absorb nutrients efficiently, sleeping is more difficult, breathing becomes shallow and labored, and muscles atrophy. Without supplemental oxygen, the climber's judgment may deteriorate significantly. The impairment is much like the effects of alcohol. The climber may recognize the hazard or risk, but can't react in time to prevent disaster. Climbers typically only have a maximum of two or three days that they can endure at that altitude, even with supplemental oxygen.

I have seen the Death Zone at the higher altitudes on the Mountain of God. The zeal and strength of the flesh atrophies and dies as I move higher into His Presence. Up there I am more aware of how even seemingly minor weaknesses or faults become critical impediments to moving higher. The flesh can't survive there.

And, the more excruciating for the flesh, the more the spirit can soar! I have discovered what it means to mount up with wings as eagles. Up there, I and others have lost our appetite for the things of this world and we were no longer bound by the lowland pursuits. That altitude allowed us to taste real freedom. I want to walk in the spiritual Death Zone regularly. Those who yearn to live a holy life can find a welcome into the presence of His holy fire; I've seen that one can even be comfortable there. Up there, the creativity, energy, and efficiency of being led by the Holy Spirit bring *unearthly* power.

And the impact I have is far greater than I could ever have relying on my own strength and abilities. I want to live where my "natural judgment" is impaired; I want to live in and by the power of the Holy Spirit. I want to be so critically dependent upon Him I cannot function effectively without His direct involvement.

When I have found that place, I relied upon the Spirit to accomplish His purpose; it was awesome to see the impact in people; I spoke "His words to His people" (Jeremiah 23:22). But when I moved on my own, what I shared came across as "*my* words to His people." I sounded foolish, simple-minded, dense, and just plain stupid. My impaired spiritual judgment was plain for all to see.

The Descent

Most high-altitude climbing disasters happen on the way *down*. All the reasons are related to a few simple issues: 1) exposure to extreme conditions for a long time, 2) the climbers have stayed out too long and darkness overtakes them, and 3) lack of sufficient food and drink; climbers are running on an empty tank. We must be diligent to not to let our focus lapse just because we reached the summit and are longing for shelter, warmth, and safety.

How many of us have stumbled and fallen so quickly after a spiritual or ministry high point? How many Christian leaders get tripped up after finally achieving something great for God? Remember, "getting to the top is optional, getting down safely is mandatory." Some very simple steps can help you get back down safely after a high point. During the ascent, climbers frequently leave a stash of simple food and additional oxygen bottles at a convenient place so they can quickly replenish on the way down. So as you ascend to a spiritual high place, make arrangements for your replenishment on the descent. Find a place to worship privately, feed yourself on His

Word, and get together with your Base Camp for prayer and good counsel. Celebrate and enjoy the summit, but re-focus so that as you descend you have the reserves and vision to make it home.

Rest and Recuperation

Beyond the replenishment for the descent, mountaineers also need to get back to camp where they can rest long enough for God to restore deep reserves that have been burned up in the climb. He may also want you to rest so that the things He showed you up high can settle and clarify.

During a two- to three-month expedition on Everest, climbers can lose up to 40 pounds. After the expedition, they'll go back down to low elevation, eat, sleep, and rest until they've recuperated. It can take weeks. Only rarely will high-altitude climbers schedule back-to-back climbs. Spiritual Mountaineers should learn from them. Jesus, Himself, withdrew regularly from the challenge of public ministry to replenish Himself. Take time to rest and recuperate before you get back into the work of God again. The recuperation must be sufficient to recharge your reserves. It may take an hour, a day, weeks, or months. But then get back out there and impact your world. Don't turn into someone that just hangs around the "spiritual hot tub" all the time.

Finally, I've also learned that we can trust Him to develop and acclimate us for that high call. We can be patient with His timeline; sometimes He calls us to a brute force march, and sometimes He calls us to rest back at Base Camp. Take the long view; you're on a lifelong *expedition* to the summit. It's not a sprint.

CHAPTER 12

DANGERS, RISKS, AND SUFFERING

....

Those who remain in their comfort zones do not climb mountains. Danger lies in wait on every step up on the high snow- and ice-covered ridges. The difference between life and death can be as thin as a 13mm rope. The high reaches of Denali feature some of the worst weather on the planet. Above 20,000′ on any mountain can be a harsh, inhospitable, and unforgiving place. Up there, even the simplest error, one that would be inconsequential at lower altitudes, can put a mountaineer's life on or past the ragged edge. High-altitude climbers understand those risks and work within them to reach places few people ever see.

Just like the high-altitude climber, Spiritual Mountaineers must recognize the risks and dangers, be able to account for them, and press past them toward the call of the mountain. Mountaineers must be able to deal with storms, the risks of exposure, simple mistakes and falls, avalanches, crevasses, etc. They must manage the risks to prevent disaster and achieve their summit.

Storms and Spiritual Meteorology

One of the most frequent causes of mountaineering disasters is misreading the early warning signs of storms. Climbers make incredible investments to get a shot at a summit, but that can create a blind push for some achievement they've dreamed about for years. By missing the indicators, climbers can push themselves too far, too high, and for too long. When the storm comes on too quickly, they get caught in extremely hostile and dangerous conditions which slow the climber's descent and can set up a cascade of factors that raise the risk level beyond critical, as Mark Duggin and Brad Davidson found on their Rainier climb.

Previously, I mentioned the May 1996 disaster on Everest. Two commercial climbing teams pushed for the summit of Mount Everest. Aside from the two team leaders, many of the climbers had little high-altitude experience. Both teams had set a mandatory turnaround time of 2 pm—no matter where a climber was on the mountain, they were to turn back, even if they were less than 100 feet from the summit.

Incredibly, the very experienced guides did not enforce the turnback time or recognize the early signs of a fierce storm coming up the flanks of the mountain. In fact, they stayed above 28,000′ until late afternoon. Many got caught in a brutal storm as night fell. Eight died, including the two team leaders. They were among the most highly regarded climbers in the world, but the inability to see the early signs of the storm and lack of objective analysis took them out.

Similar factors came into play in May 2019 on Mount Everest, when a "traffic jam" of climbers led to 12 deaths. Human mania or zeal during a climb can completely wipe out the great investment of time and preparation that got the climbers there.

Spiritual Mountaineers face similar challenges.

Meteorologists study general global conditions to determine the broad patterns and trends that may affect regional and local weather. From that, they develop a detailed evaluation of current regional and local conditions. They use that to forecast the local weather. I think we could use similar principles to discern and react to spiritual storms and mitigate the negative effects.

Dangers and Risks

Risk factors create the circumstances that permit bad things to happen. Let's consider a few practical parallels between mountain climbing and Spiritual Mountaineering risks.

Weariness

Weariness is often a root cause of mountaineering disasters. Sometimes long periods of peak exertion simply leave the climber "running on empty." Perhaps the push to reach the summit brought physical and mental exhaustion. Then, they didn't have the reserves for the descent. More on that later. The same applies in Spiritual Mountaineering.

Isolation and Loss of Communication

In the disaster on Everest in 1996, climbers got isolated from each other. At that point, those who were stranded could not draw on the reserves or resources of other climbers. They lost their way. No one was there to push them and keep them focused and moving. After a while they just gave up and drifted off to a slow, cold death.

The same thing happens when Christians get isolated from one another. One reason we "do not forsake the assembling of ourselves together," (Hebrews 10:25) is because of the strength, support, and sustenance in numbers. Isolation makes us vulnerable. We should all work to maintain strong, healthy relationships and clear and frequent communication with our rope team and Base Camp. For example, don't let offenses or bitterness with your family, church family, or your team fester. Resolve things quickly and completely.

Most importantly, don't allow anything to create a distance between you and God. Run to Him as soon as you know something is wrong. Practice Hebrews 4:14-16 on a real-time basis.

Hypothermia

Long-term exposure to cold and or wet conditions can bring hypothermia. That is when your core body temperature drops too low, leading to impaired judgment, slowed thinking, slurred speech, and disorientation. Impaired judgment can cause disaster. Prolonged hypothermia will kill you. That requires getting the climber to safety, warm food, and dry, warm clothes. Very often, the victim does not recognize the signs.

We should treat spiritual hypothermia in much the same way. Those close to hypothermia victims may need to forcefully intervene to get the victim to a place of spiritual warmth, safety, and nourishment. Sometimes, just being there will let the warmth of human presence restore hope and relationships. One of the core principles of Hope Force International: *practice the ministry of presence.* Just being there demonstrating the love, mercy, and kindness of God in the flesh brings profound impact.

Loss of Balance

A simple loss of balance on a mountain can cause a little slip with an easy recovery or it can bring disaster. The ability of the climber to maintain balance in the face of distractions and extraordinary hazards is critical in high altitude climbing. The margin for error on a very high exposed section of your climb may only be a few inches.

Those who ascend the Mountain of God also have serious challenges with balance. We must balance family, professional, personal, and ministry needs. We've all known about Christian leaders who suffered moral, financial, or physical collapses because their personal lives were not in balance. You can't skip core responsibilities on the path to achieving your dream. As Stephen Covey said, "Private victory precedes public victory."[10]

Mistakes

Every year, the American Alpine Club and the Alpine Club of Canada publish an analysis of mountaineering accidents. The three most common causes of mountaineering accidents are 1) climbing un-roped, 2) attempting a climb that exceeds ability, and 3) not being adequately equipped or prepared for the situations or conditions (such as storms). They conclude that most accidents on mountains result from human error. Mistakes can mean life or death at high altitude.

Marty Hoey died on Everest in 1982 because she did not tie the end of the climbing harness strap back through the safety loop on her harness. Further, she did not ask her climbing partners to do a safety check on her before they set out that day. In the Death Zone, even the simplest error can end your climb and perhaps your life. Losing your glove, for example, may be no big deal at low elevations. But, up there your hand could freeze in two minutes. And you can't descend

---

[10] Stephen R. Covey, *The 7 Habits of Highly Effective People* (New York; Simon & Schuster, 2004)

back down the mountain without both hands. Simply catching a crampon or a strap on something can pitch a climber into a fall.

Avalanches and Crevasses

When I walked into my office Monday, September 10, 2001, I learned my job had been eliminated. AVALANCHE! It seemed like everything I thought was solid broke loose. Avalanches happen when a section of the snowpack, rock, earth, or glacier becomes unstable and breaks loose. Climbers can be caught in the path of an avalanche or may trigger one from above. The force of tons of ice and snow crashing down can be deadly.

Crevasses—big cracks in glaciers—can be huge, over half a mile long and hundreds of feet deep. The exposed and open ones are not the worst hazard (unless you misstep or slide into one). The more dangerous ones are snow bridges, a crevasse covered by a layer of snow. A climber may never realize he or she is walking over a gaping cavity in the glacier until the snow bridge drops out and the climber falls into the abyss.

Similar things can happen for the spiritual climber. Sometimes, what they thought was solid, reliable ground suddenly collapses.

Falls

Any of the dangers I've mentioned can trigger a fall. If you don't know how to stop quickly, you can suddenly find yourself 100 feet down the slope and gaining speed rapidly. The further and faster you go increases the likelihood of a bad outcome.

In addition, one person's fall can take the whole team out if they don't recognize what is happening and take immediate action to stop it. For that reason, one of the most important parts of our Rainier training was on how to stop falls. "Self-arrest" and "team-arrest" techniques are critically important on a climb. Any fall must be stopped as quickly as possible. Our training stressed two key points about falls:

1. Climbers should yell, "FALLING!" as loud as possible. That is essential so that the other people on the rope team can get down in the arrest position before the rope goes taut, to stop the fall and keep everyone from getting ripped off the mountain.[11]
2. Each climber must do everything possible to stop the fall quickly. The guides taught us how to stop with and without an ice axe. Self-arrest with an ice axe is a very specific, choreographed maneuver that can stop you very quickly. It isn't pretty or graceful, but it does the job. Stopping is more important than how well you executed the proper technique. Bottom line, stop!

Spiritual Mountaineers must understand and apply the same principles. Sadly, too often falling brings shame. So, we don't yell, "falling." And often the last place we think of going is to our local church family.

If you fall, do whatever it takes to get back to solid ground. That may require help from others to pull you out of the crevasse or dig you out from the avalanche debris. The principles are the same as with other dangers and risks. Call for help and get back to stable ground, safety, nourishment, warmth, and shelter as fast as you can.

---

11 That was the case on Mt. Hood in May of 2002 as three climbing teams descended from the summit. On a particularly steep and difficult pitch, the highest climber on the uphill team lost his footing. Before any on his team knew what happened, he rocketed by them and ripped the entire team off the slope. As they flew down the icy face, they took out the two other teams below them. They did not stop until they dropped into a crevasse some 500 feet below. Five died.

Almost immediately after I got home with my box of personal things the morning of September 10, 2001, I reached out to friends for prayer. The stabilizing effect was immediate. I soon recognized that what felt like a gut punch of losing something I relied on was actually a launching pad.

A simple, practical example of how I react to falls is whenever I feel the pressure of significant spiritual resistance or just battle fatigue, I send a quick text to trusted friends. I don't get into the details of the struggle. Often, it's just: "Hey, I'm feeling some headwinds (or worse, really struggling with some things), could use your prayer support today."

If we understand God's heart and our own frailties, we will recognize that temptations are common to man (1 Corinthians 10:13). Jesus said *we would* have tribulation in this world. So, it should be our nature to urgently call out to God (as in Hebrews 4:15) and our fellow climbers for help. Obviously, any fall carries serious implications for the whole team (including the family). That's why the team must move quickly and decisively. They must forget the routine and the business-as-usual, and move quickly to save a life.

Prevention

We are not able to know every strategy and tactic of the devil. His imagination, creativity, and scope in the spiritual realm are far beyond what we can comprehend with the natural mind or sense in our spirit. But a few basic skills are essential to helping you recognize and prevent storms. They all reflect the basic training and team concepts of mountaineers that we've discussed throughout this book:

1. Stay spiritually fit: We must maintain the basic disciplines of a spiritually fit life. High-altitude mountaineers, physical or spiritual, must maintain a very high level of personal fitness. This can't be overstated.

2. Stay connected to your guide: avoid anything that could compromise or sever your real-time connection with the Holy Spirit. You just can't afford the consequences if you are pushing for a high summit.
3. Stay connected to your rope team and Base Camp: Surround yourself with a solid team. They must be able to objectively evaluate how you are doing, give you frank feedback, keep you from falling, and launch a rescue if you go down. You were never meant to do this alone.
4. Understand root cause: Learn to see a storm for what it really is. When storms rage, we often mistake who or what the real enemy is and direct our frustration or anger at the tools he used rather than the true enemy. If we recognize the real enemy, we can deal with the situation properly, pray more effectively, and avoid doing collateral damage.
5. Develop the ability to recognize and respond to the early warning signs of approaching storms. Spiritual Mountaineers can never become casual about approaching storms and linger too long in an exposed position. The key is recognizing the progression early enough to cut it off before it becomes a raging storm and get to a place of spiritual safety and shelter before it hits full force.
6. The bottom line: Prevention involves a regular habit of examining what you are standing on or hanging from. Don't take anyone's word for it. Scrutinize every inch of the surface you will cover. Study your equipment, your assumptions and expectations, and even the foundations for your life and actions. Validate everything before you go. Seek wise counsel from trusted advisers who are willing to get in your business. Prepare yourself; be sober of spirit, be on the alert. Your adversary, the

devil, prowls about like a roaring lion, seeking someone to devour (1 Peter 5:8).

Survival

Get to Safety. In a storm, the most immediate issue is to get to shelter, safety, warmth, and nourishment. Sometimes that means getting back to a lower camp or even Base Camp to regain strength. In absolute emergencies at high altitudes, like what Mark Duggin and Brad Davidson encountered, climbers may dig a cave in the snow and hole up until the storm passes. The only focus is to simply survive! Hunker down and focus on the basics (reading, prayer, fasting, fellowship with mature believers, etc.) Call for prayer. Just hole up with God and trusted believers until the storm passes.

The Value of Suffering and Hardship

I know God allows hardship and storms just to force us to hunker down, go back to basics, and rest while we wait out the storm. Sometimes He allows the storms in order to strengthen us for what lies up higher. Scripture is very clear about the value of suffering in our lives and how it is actually central to our development. God also uses suffering to

- teach us obedience, compassion, humility, and gratefulness
- make us interdependent,
- remove presumption and arrogance
- it yields the peaceful fruit of righteousness
- to perfect us

He goes so far as to say if we don't suffer hardship, we are not legitimate sons of God. The bottom line: Suffering disconnects us from our reliance on the things of this world.

Remember, asking God to remove the difficulties and trials in life is like a hurdler asking his coach to remove the hurdles in practice. If the point of trials and difficulties is to train and strengthen us, why would we cry out to have them removed? We must be able to effectively deal with storms; we just can't be fair weather Christians.

CHAPTER 13

FOCUS, DETERMINATION, AND RISK MANAGEMENT

....

THEREFORE, SINCE WE HAVE SO GREAT A CLOUD OF WITNESSES surrounding us, let us also lay aside every encumbrance, and the sin which so easily entangles us. And let us run with endurance the race set before us, fixing our eyes on Jesus, the author and perfecter of our faith, who for the joy set before Him endured the cross, despising the shame, and has sat down at the right hand of the throne of God. For consider Him who has endured such hostility by sinners against Himself, so that you may not grow weary and lose heart. You have not yet resisted to the point of shedding blood in your striving against sin... HEBREWS 12:1-4

We have all heard the stories about professional athletes or others at the top of their field who push through distractions and pain to achieve greatness. Their focus and drive seem beyond what ordinary people possess. Who can forget Kerri Strug, the young gymnast who won the 1996 US Olympic women's team competition for the US with that unbelievable vault on a fractured ankle? And, she had to sprint on that ankle to get to the vault!

Alex Van Steen, a career mountain guide, explains it as building a house of pain. Each experience builds our ability to deal with pain or difficulty. Over time, we build a house that will stand the test of serious storms. Krzysztof Wielicki, one of the world's most successful Himalayan mountaineers, describes it as "the joy of positive suffering-because if something is easy, you will not enjoy it, really."

You can feel that kind of seasoning when you are around people who have been through extraordinary hardship such as the Holocaust, horrific accidents, long and grueling seasons of painful illness, or other crucibles. They have an incredible depth of character. Why is that? I think it's because they went through something that stripped away all of the stuff of life and left the real person – no veils, no props. They were reduced to the real deal. Their heart was left with only what really matters.

Read the personal accounts of high-altitude climbers; so many recall the long, slow struggles on summit day – everything in their body screams to stop and turn around. The legs are rubber, the lungs burn, the mind discourages… *"what are you doing here… you could die out here… the wind feels like needles on my face…. Man, it's cold… I've never felt cold like this… Is my eye frozen shut…Will I lose my toes or fingers?*

But, the climber also knows to fight back against the mental discouragement…"*the top is not far; I've got to press on… one foot down, rest, breathe, move the other foot forward, rest, breathe, do it again, do it again… just keep moving; if I stop I'll die… "* That is how to push toward the mark of the upward call. The great mountaineers get so focused on the summit that distractions have no effect. They concentrate on achieving, not avoiding.

Do you remember the story about Joe Simpson in Chapter 9? His unyielding focus on survival is one of the most extraordinary examples of determination I've ever heard. For Joe, there was no option to bail out when things got tough.

When England was being pounded by German bombing missions in World War II, Winston Churchill gave his famous call: "Never give in. Never give in. Never, never, never, never—in nothing, great or small, large or petty—never give in, except to convictions of honor and good sense. Never yield to force. Never yield to the apparently overwhelming might of the enemy."

High altitudes are basically inhospitable places. Not enough oxygen to maintain life, no water, extremely cold temperatures, and then the wind... Walking the high places with God on this earth are much the same. We are driven by a force that this world doesn't understand, doesn't appreciate, and our objectives are completely contrary to the wind of the prevailing wisdom. Reaching a spiritual summit requires strong focus and drive, commitment, determination, endurance, wisdom, and judgment.

Stephen Covey said, "The main thing is to keep the main thing the main thing."[12] What does that mean? Almost every minute of every day bombards us with things that will blow us off course if we are not focused. We must fight to stay on point.

One of my favorite hymns is "Rise Up O Men of God." The first line is: "Rise up o men of God, have done with lesser things, give heart and soul and mind and strength to serve the King of Kings."[13]

The "lesser things" are anything that keeps us from a simple focus on mission-critical objectives; things that are essential for the climb

---

12 Stephen R. Covey, *First Things First* (New York; Simon & Schuster, 1994).
13 William P. Merrill, *Rise Up O Men of God,* Public domain.

and nothing else. We are often distracted from pursuing God by good, but lesser, things. Maturity calls us to carefully evaluate where our spiritual energy and time get spent. Jesus is the best model of focus, determination, and mental toughness in all of history. Isaiah understood it; he foretold Jesus' purposeful intention: "Therefore, I have set my face like flint, and I know I shall not be ashamed." (Isaiah 50:7). Nothing and no one could pull Him off course.

Think about what Paul wrote about being dead to sin (Romans 6:11). What does it mean? If you go down to the morgue, pull a body out of the cold box and run any kind of temptation at it, what reaction will you get? What if you spewed out abusive and demeaning insults? What if you tempted it with money or sex? What reaction would you get? "He" would not hide his face or recite verses in order to stay strong. That is what "dead to sin" means. No reaction. Nothing. Dead.

Natural and Spiritual Mountaineering taught me to train my mind, renew my mind, and take every thought captive (2 Corinthians 10:5 and Philippians 4:8). We need to be tough to handle what we encounter every day. We must develop the ability to deal with difficult people, decisions, and situations. Climbing high on the Mountain of God requires an absolute, unyielding, unwavering focus on Christ (Hebrews 12:1-4). Peter walked on water as long as he kept his focus on Jesus; when he took his eyes off the Lord, he started to sink. If we fix our eyes on Him, God will carry us through the dangers we face and lead us to the high places with Him. In Spiritual Mountaineering, each challenge increases your capacity to climb and prepares you for the high places in God. If God's call is contrary to the course of this world, then we will always be pushing upstream. Always. Everything in this world is set up to work against our fulfilling the call.

Ask God to show you what are truly distractions in your life. Ask Him to teach you how to recognize lesser things, distractions, and sin and then submit yourself to His training ground. It's not some legalistic thing at all. It's a matter of relative priorities. How badly do you want the high places of God? Sometimes we must dig much deeper than we thought possible to set our face into the wind and press on. When the wind blows harder, I will tighten my straps, pull in all loose ends, set my feet, lean into the wind, and press on. When it comes down to the gut-level will to make it, I *refuse* to lie down and die. *I will not yield.* I will stand in the storm when all others run for cover. Outside of God, no one will take me out. No one.

Risk Management/Face Your Fears

Understanding the inherent risks involved in any activity is vital in viewing it with proper respect and reality. Mountaineering is certainly no different, and wearing rose-colored glasses in your preparation phase is detrimental to the overall experience of the journey.

Climbing exposes you to a wide range of risks, many of which could end your life. Spiritual Mountaineering presents its own unique risks. Depending on how you handle them, they could end your spiritual life or disable you to the extent that you may not reach your potential. In the face of risks and dangers, some run for cover. Some set the course of their lives to avoid risk at all costs. C.T. Studd, a 19th-century missionary, reportedly said: "I do not wish to live 'neath sound of church or chapel bell; I want to run a rescue shop within a yard of hell." He recognized the danger, counted the cost, and moved ahead in spite of it.

If you try to avoid every danger in life, you may find that you did not have much of a life at all. Risk cannot be avoided, but can be managed. Mountaineer Lou Whittaker reportedly said, "Fear does not keep me from climbing; rather it keeps me alert enough to the dangers that I am careful and am always thinking of contingency plans. That is why I survive." Ultimately, it's about risk management. In food and pharmaceutical operations, we are trained in Hazard Analysis and Critical Control Points (HACCP). We are trained to evaluate situations, processes, and equipment to identify the potential hazards and the factors critical in determining the outcome. The first four steps are:

1. Conduct a Hazard Analysis: List the points or steps in the process where significant hazards are likely to occur.
2. Identify the Critical Control Points (CCPs): Determine which of those points, steps, or procedures can be controlled to prevent or eliminate negative outcomes?
3. Establish Critical Limits: Determine operating ranges (critical limits) for each Critical Control Point (to verify that operating within those ranges will prevent, eliminate, or reduce the likelihood of occurrence for the potential hazard to an acceptable level).
4. Monitor the CCPs: The HACCP team will describe monitoring procedures for the measurement of the critical limit at each critical control point.

That is precisely how Spiritual Mountaineers should approach risk management. Count the cost as in Luke 14:25-33. Determine where you can take properly calculated risks (recall the discussion of the top-flight athletes or race car drivers who determine where they can push the limits of their abilities), The monitoring is done largely by your rope team and Base Camp. We just won't avoid disaster without critical objective input.

Danger does not keep climbers from pushing for higher ground. They just take precautions, prepare for changes, and respond to surprises quickly and effectively. In the same way, Christians count the cost, die to self, and forget what lies behind in order to press on to the upward call of God in Christ Jesus (Philippians 3:13-14). That's what being a Spiritual Mountaineer means. That should be a mark of a Christian; we should be stable and fixed on the goal in the midst of situations that would take others out.

Assess the dangers, put proper controls, protections, and boundaries in place, but then stand in the storm; set your feet, face the wind, and lean in (Eph 6:10-18) That is true courage.

CHAPTER 14

MOUNTAIN RESCUE AND DISASTER RESPONSE

....

"Brethren, even if a man is caught in any trespass, you who are spiritual, restore such a one in the spirit of gentleness; each one of you looking to yourself, lest you too be tempted. Bear one another's burdens, and thus fulfill the law of Christ."
– GALATIANS 6: 1, 2

....

CLIMBING MOUNTAINS IS ONE OF THE MOST DANGEROUS things people do. Life insurance companies do not offer coverage for mountaineers. The risks are too high.

So, what happens when a climber goes down? First, the other teams on the mountain immediately shift their priorities to saving the fallen climber or team. Those who are called into a rescue must be very proficient climbers, trained in all aspects of first aid, disaster response, exposure, etc. But a trained mountain rescuer told me the most significant thing is they must be prepared for whatever they might find when they get to the climber. They may find someone who is lost or disoriented, immobilized or injured. They may find a dead body. Every rescue team heads off into the teeth of disaster, intent on bringing back those who are lost, hurt, or worse. They put their lives in danger to save another.

Tough work, but they do it because it is the right thing—the only thing—to do. As examples of the Golden Rule, they do for others what they would want done for them. They get out there and snatch lives from the brink.

In spite of how long they have dreamed, planned, and trained for their summit bid, they do whatever it takes to save a lost climber and get them back safely to Base Camp.

Unfortunately, Christians are not very good at rescue. Sure, we tell people we'll pray for them, and may even follow through, but rescues are really inconvenient. The timing almost never fits our agenda How many times have we wondered about people who have gone off radar? We're often just too busy to track them down and launch a rescue if necessary. Then we later hear that the bottom fell out on them. Several friends have lived this scenario over the last few years; some have totally checked out on God or any hope of His call for their lives. It is gut-wrenching to watch. I feel the enemy has stolen some lifelong friends. I wish, with all my heart, I had made more of an effort to intervene.

We must all learn to recognize the indicators of a climber at risk. We need to be trained on how to handle tough situations, be prepared for whatever we may find, know how to discern the warnings of the Holy Spirit before disaster strikes, and if necessary, confront a brother or sister in love before they go down. Rescuers must be prepared to give orders and take charge. A climber may be in bad shape, while insisting he is fine, as Mark and Brad did on their descent from the top of Rainier after the weather cleared. And when they do go down, we need to stay in the rescue until the climber is securely back to safety. They are worth the struggle and inconvenience. You may be the only one who can save them.

How Do I Do It?

My wife and I serve on the board of directors for Hope Force International, a disaster response organization. Hope Force volunteers are often among the first responders following tornados, hurricanes, floods, and earthquakes. They are trained on three phases of disaster response: Relief, Recovery, Rebuild. HFI volunteers muck out flooded houses, remove damaged belongings and materials, rebuild homes and, therefore, peoples' lives. HFI volunteers help people recover when disaster strikes.

One of the core principles for HFI is practice the ministry of presence. *Just be there* for someone whose life has been devastated. Demonstrate warmth, care, and compassion to bring hope to those affected by crisis or disaster. The parallels with mountain rescue are strong.

We can also take some lessons from mountain rescue principles. First, the decisions made immediately following an incident set the course for the outcome.

Assessment is the first action. Rescue efforts must quickly evaluate the situation. Mountaineers consider weather, snow conditions, location and position of the climber, what equipment and food they have at their disposal, the altitude, etc. When searching for the lost, rescue teams may have to go back to where they were last seen and look for clues of where and how they might have gotten off course or fallen.

Then work to establish communication. The injured may or may not be lucid and able to communicate. Judgment and discernment are essential to knowing how to re-establish communication, often on their terms, where they are, with no expectations about their response. Listen. Read their physical and spiritual body language. A friend who was going through a very prolonged and difficult season of despair said, "Just be here, don't try to fix me." Practice the ministry of presence.

Next step: Secure the climber. Fast. It's pretty simple. Find a way to securely anchor them to the mountain so that neither they nor you fall further during the rescue. It can be tricky because you may not have much to work with. But you have to secure them to something solid immediately. That might mean getting together regularly just to be a listening ear. It might mean more of an intervention like taking the car keys, replacing locks. But this is where the wisdom of counsel from your rope team or Base Camp can be critical. Help them get back to the foundational principles that have undergirded them in the past. As in a disaster response, you may have to remove the muck and damage.

Next, give initial treatment for injuries, exposure, and malnourishment. Diagnose where they are hurt and treat accordingly. The same spiritual sensitivity and judgment come into play here. Listen. Minister life, hope, peace, faith, love. Be sensitive, be real. Don't bother with Christian platitudes. As we are told in Galatians 6:10, "Restore with a spirit of gentleness."

When everything has unraveled in someone's life, he or she may need help to just focus on healing and restoring the easy things first. When they get some sense of solid footing, they can tackle the big stuff. Just let them sit for a little while until they have the strength and a more stable foundation. Minimize the potential for additional damage, but let them rest until they are ready and resources are available to deal properly with the issues.

Develop a recovery plan. This includes getting the injured back to safety (Base Camp hospital). Then determine what medium- and long-range help and supports are required to restore the climber to full health and strength. Maybe they need weekly meetings for fellowship, mentoring, coaching, and discipleship. *This* is the stage to examine how the accident happened, and the time to equip the climber with the skills, support, tools, etc. to prevent the same from happening in the future. He may need an accountability mechanism or training on how to properly study the Bible. Press into God, be transparent, be committed, and allow the Holy Spirit to guide the process.

Implement the Plan. This may involve a real commitment from the rescuer to be there long enough for a true rebuild (as in the Hope Force process).

Don't rush it. Full restoration can take a long time. It may inconvenience the rescue team, but it is critically important. Getting back on the mountain to climb prematurely is a setup for total disaster.

A Missed Rescue

A good friend went to Ukraine as an independent missionary in the early '90s. He heard God's call but went with no real planning. He did not establish a full, solid support team before leaving, no real Base Camp or rope team. He just packed up his wife and kids and went. After all, the need was great and the cry for help from the former Soviet Republic was urgent.

He pushed ahead tirelessly for nearly 10 years. No vacation or furlough; "Too much to do." Over the years he and his wife planted many churches, most of which are still running today. Ultimately, he led a coalition of at least 40 churches; he served as a pastor to pastors in addition to pastoring a church himself. The ministry purchased a former communist retreat center and converted it to a summer camp, retreat center, and training center to develop Ukrainian pastors and missionaries. Lots of really great stuff.

But, because he did not build an adequate Base Camp of support people here, he was isolated and exposed. And what little support they once had faded over time. In desperation, he asked me to take the lead in re-assembling the US support team (the ministry board). He wanted me to help with the growing administrative burden. But I was busy with my young family and growing responsibilities at work. So, I didn't recognize the nature of the call and therefore the urgency of the need. I did not sense the seriousness of the danger he and his wife were facing. They had been out in the wilderness, at high altitude, and had experienced long-term exposure to the storms and other elements – isolation, spiritual hypothermia, lack of adequate spiritual nutrition and prayer support. The result was impaired judgment about how to continue to grow and develop the ministry, when to take a break, etc. I didn't recognize those signs either.

They kept pushing, faithfully serving their flock in the midst of the storm and long-term exposure. They stayed on the mountain too long. Finally, burned out, they returned to the US, crawled in a hole and stayed there for nearly a year. I finally tracked them down and did help them back to solid ground. In time, they recovered. Today, they are back in the ministry and have a much deeper appreciation for support, good judgment, and a balance between the needs of others and their own personal needs.

What should I have done differently? Perhaps nothing. I had my own family and career responsibilities. We were both doing what we thought was right at the time and God was blessing what we both put our hand to. But I do wish that I – or somebody – had been able to help when they called out the first time. They needed someone to call them regularly, pray faithfully, and take other actions in support of them and their ministry. Someone needed to tell them directly when it was time to come back for a break and to make sure they got proper food and nourishment once they finally stumbled back to Base Camp.

Humans have frailties, and life is hazardous. Anyone can fall or get injured. So rescue and recovery will always be essential skills. Mountain climbers understand that. They will put their own lives on hold, disregard the money they paid for the adventure, and throw themselves into rescuing those in trouble.

I wish the church could be that serious, selfless, intelligent, and disciplined about rescues. People who are dying or hurting aren't very polite and don't care about your schedule (neither does God). At the moment of need, those in need of rescue could not care less about your calendar or your convenience.

It is time for the church to rethink our approach to rescue and recovery.

That is the ultimate point of mountaineering: Living and striving in faithful interdependence and partnership with the others on the mountain. That provides a clear and accurate framework for viewing our role and purpose in this life.

Part 3

....

LEAVING A LEGACY

*I*F SPIRITUAL MOUNTAINEERING MEANS ANYTHING AT ALL, IT must build entrance and influence for those who will come after us. We have to train others who can climb summits we've never seen. Often God gives us dreams that are for others to fulfill. We build the foundation upon which they stand to fulfill the dream. And they do the same for those who follow. Moses led Israel to the Promised Land, but Joshua led them in. David dreamed of a permanent temple for God, but Solomon built it. So, in this last section, we will consider the great wisdom and beauty in how God helps us to build and leave a legacy.

CHAPTER 15

A HEART FOR UNNAMED PEAKS

....

*I*AND MANY LEADERS SHARE A CONCERN ABOUT THE WAY THE church in America sees and preaches the gospel. Many have lamented that we seem to have been evangelized by *business-think*. We increasingly think in marketing language and ideas. What's the benefit for the customer? How can we sell the sizzle? Can we create desire for something new?

But, Jesus said, "...Whoever wishes to save his life shall lose it, but whoever loses his life for My sake, he is the one who will save it." (Luke 9:24, Matthew 10:39 and 16:25) We are called to *His* purpose, not our own. The Kingdom of God represents His plan for the universe, not mine.

So, how does that affect the way we walk with Him?

Ever wonder why the famous mountain peaks draw so many climbers? Because conquering those summits gives notoriety, even celebrity status, to those who can afford to pay for adrenaline tours. A 2019 *New York Times* article reported the increasing crowds on Mount Everest, a surge that has produced more dangerous adventures. Here's how Times reporters described the situation:

"Climbers were pushing and shoving to take selfies. The flat part of the summit, which he estimated at about the size of two Ping-Pong tables, was packed with 15 or 20 people. To get up there, he had to wait hours in a line, chest to chest, one puffy jacket after the next, on an icy, rocky ridge with a several-thousand-foot drop. He even had to step around the body of a woman who had just died." [14]

But that has nothing to do with the timeless quest to reach far beyond life's lowlands. We cannot compare the desire to be famous for climbing a peak with responding to the ancient call of the mountain. A true mountaineer will grapple with a mountain that holds no fame at all. It's about the climb, not the press release.

In the same way, God calls us to His majestic and eternal purposes, not our own reality show. Yet, Christian culture too often conforms to the dominant culture's thirst for fame. That's why most Christians know about Billy Graham, Lou Engle, Jack Hayford, T.D. Jakes, Lauren Daigle, or Steven Curtis Chapman. Naturally, I thank God each of those famous Christians have excellent reputations for integrity and excellence of spirit. Still, many immature Christians want to be like them more than they want to be like Christ.

The Apostle Paul spoke of being "in labor until Christ is formed in you" (Galatians 4:19). That mysterious process does not produce notoriety; it impregnates people with the Spirit of Christ. I could name hundreds of people unknown to you, but each of them knows

---

[14] Kai Schultz, Jeffrey Gettleman, Mujib Mashal and Bhadra Sharma. *'It Was Like a Zoo': Death on an Unruly, Overcrowded Everest.* The New York Times, May 29, 2019. https://www.nytimes.com/2019/05/26/world/asia/mount-everest-deaths.html

the profound reality of Christ being formed within. They have a heart for the unknown peaks within God's vast kingdom.

Many of us—in fact, *most* of us—have been called to tasks or roles that will never be in the public eye, have press releases, or receive attention from media or grantmaking foundations. Sometimes the nameless peaks represent the hardest climbs. Some are not mapped, certainly not in the spotlight and, therefore, never get the support or recognition given to the high-profile, recognized peaks (such as the jobs of famous Christian athletes, politicians, and entertainers). The unnamed peaks roles—like public servant, truck driver, elementary school PE teacher, file clerk, hairdresser, etc.—climb alone. No one notices but God and maybe a small Base Camp. Of course, He who sees in secret will reward those climbers.

Take a mom for example: She slogs through the daily grind of house cleaning and maintenance, meal planning, juggling kids' schedules, and doctor appointments. Then one day, after the cat pooped on the living room floor again, the kids left their toilet clogged, the pile of laundry kept growing, and her 13-year-old daughter hits the door at 2:43 p.m. after a horrible day, God says "I need you now!" He needs to speak through the mom, to say things that will change the course of her daughter's life forever. Will the mom be ready?

But just because others may not understand why you climb does not mean your call is illegitimate. God often calls His children to break fresh ground, to blaze a trail where there is no paved road.

Where is your peak? Is it the barren wilderness of the ghetto or barrio or American suburbia? Managing a business that employs those with prison records? Teaching English as a Second Language to immigrants? Volunteering to hold babies born with drug addictions? Dig deep. Press hard for the trail markers and a picture of the call. God will reveal it to those who are serious enough to make the climb.

Those who have proven they have a heart for the unnamed peaks can be trusted to bear His Name. That kind of person will leave a legacy that seeks first His kingdom.

CHAPTER 16

THE HEART OF THE MOUNTAINEER

*"Our society cannot survive another generation
of Christians who just fit in."*
– MICAH MCGLORY

How does our Creator see mountains? What is their purpose? Why that upward thrust? Upheaval, disruption, and struggle seem to be timeless creative forces in God's hands. Is that why mountains— like Moriah, Ararat, Nebo, Sinai, Olivet, Carmel, and others—are so prominent in scripture? Abraham had to climb Mount Moriah with his son Isaac for a meeting with God. And Moses climbed Mount Sinai to receive the tablets of the law from the Lord. He doesn't make it easy.

As I wrote earlier in this book, "You have to *overcome* mountains." Like Abraham on Moriah and Moses on Sinai, we have to climb, to work very hard to overcome those pinnacles. We cannot summit the mountain solely by attending a worship concert, reading a great book on spiritual life, giving, or fasting and praying. We have to plan, train, exert ourselves, hurt, fall, bleed, maybe give up and then get back up.

I finish this book as the whole earth is caught in the coronavirus outbreak. That virus has surely presented the largest upheaval and disruption of my life. What does that mean? Will the nations—will *I*—pursue business as usual? Or will we, people and nations, allow God to use it to lead us to higher ground? And, will we produce leaders who can function as God's representatives for summiting fresh challenges and disruptions? That is the real test for Spiritual Mountaineering.

Parkinson's: Training for the Summit

As I deal with Parkinson's, I know it forces me into focus and determination. I see the world differently because of this struggle with disease. But I've also learned that the real issues are not the struggle. It's about the outcome that accrues from that struggle. It's about what God wants to accomplish in our lives *through* the hardship. It's about where He wants to take us. Scripture is very clear: He uses hardship and suffering to perfect us and help us to touch something eternal in the call of God upon our lives. Through them we see the Lord from a fresh angle.

Climbing mountains—whether Rainier or Parkinson's—requires extraordinary effort, focus, determination, and drive. Of course, it's important to pay your bills, maintain your car, repair your house, and all those mundane things. But those aren't really what life is about. Challenges and hardships can serve God's great purposes by stripping away the junk and debris of life and separating us from our attachment to this world. Like everyone listed in Hebrews chapter 11, they weren't distracted by whether they did great exploits or lived in caves; their singular focus was on the hope that their true life was only found in God (Heb 11: 39-40).

We often hear traditionalists say they just want to hear God say, "Well done, good and faithful servant, enter into your rest." I understand and respect that statement. But, that's not what I want to hear most. I think the highest honor that could be paid to a human life is found in Hebrews 11:38: "men of whom this world was not worthy." Jesus and all who follow Him come to a point where their alignment with the Kingdom of God pulls them above the culture's approval. That is part of what total focus and exertion does for anyone seeking God.

I have worked hard on this phase of my life. In fact, six of the typical Parkinson's symptoms have actually improved. I have more freedom of movement in my left hand, left arm, and my shoulder joint. The strength I lost in my left arm is back. The pace of my stride had slowed (which is typical of Parkinson's), but that has returned to normal. My balance and coordination are much better now. The hoarseness in my voice, also a typical Parkinson's symptom, has disappeared.

I started playing hacky sack again, which is great for balance and coordination, and forcing my brain to work in those areas that govern motor control and balance. The point of all this is that I intentionally challenge my capacity and push my limits. That *pushing* is a core element of mountaineering too. Not just settling for what life hands you, but pushing hard against the resistance. I do it because God's plans, thoughts, and ways surpass all the norms of this life. And it is the only way to prepare myself to meet Him on this mountain.

My Everest

So now, after 40 years of pursuing God and driving for personal, spiritual, and professional development, I think I have finally arrived at the Base Camp for the Everest of my life. In one way, I'm a little like Caleb. The 14th chapter of Joshua paints a beautiful picture of him asking Joshua to give him "this mountain" so he can conquer it, driving out the enemies. He said, "I am 85 years old today, I am still as strong as I was in the day Moses sent me; as my strength was then, so my strength is now." (Joshua 14: 10-11)

That faithful man never wavered in the unbelief that destroyed so many others around him. So, he basically told Israel's leader, "Hey, Joshua, today is my birthday; would you give me a birthday present—that land I first saw 45 years ago?"

As the founder and CEO of a pharmaceutical company, I stand before a land I first saw almost four decades ago. And I want to be like Caleb, earnestly seeking ownership of that "mountain" of possibilities. I now stand here because of my Parkinson's diagnosis. If that hadn't happened, I wouldn't have reached this Promised Land. Is it too big a dream to think our work could profoundly change the lives of those who deal with major neurodegenerative disorders? Caleb summed up his request to Joshua by saying, "Perhaps the Lord will be with me, and I shall drive them out as the Lord has spoken." Yes, I agree. *Perhaps* the Lord will help me conquer what He let me see so long ago.

In the last 10 years, God has coordinated events, connections, and relationships more frequently and in stranger ways than I've ever seen. Standing where I do now, I often feel as if I am on a high exposed ridge on Everest. The risks and implications of failure or just a simple misstep are more critical than I've ever known in my life.

It's almost indescribable. At 61, I see more clearly and feel more alive, energized, and excited about the future than ever before in my life.

How did I get here? For most of my life I have had a low-level discontent about the way things were.

When I first became a Christian, I had hope for a grand and exciting future, but real life didn't seem to reflect that potential. I didn't see in the church what I saw in the Bible. I mean, did the

Bible say we could do greater works than Christ did? And what does it really mean to be "led by the Spirit" or to walk in the world but not be of the world? Would we really see His kingdom come here on earth and what would that look like? What does it mean to be a light to darkness?

Somewhere along the way I realized that if God is Who He says He is: knows all things, sees all things, knows the beginning and the end, has all power, and loves me far more than I can ever understand, then not fully surrendering my life to Him is the single most illogical decision I could ever make. My entire life since then has been about learning and implementing the principles of this book. All my life I have been hoping for a place I've never been.

Those questions frame up my life's preparation. I wanted to be a vessel He could use. I tried to pursue righteousness, emptying myself as passionately as possible, surrendering everything that I was. I've tried to hear His voice, practice obedience even in the smallest things, walk in humility before Him. I want to know Him and be known by Him. As I progressed through personal and professional development, I pressed to learn about leadership, stewardship, and how to have a lasting positive impact. The bottom line is that I have long wanted to push the limits of my mental, spiritual, and physical capacity as far as possible, so I did not limit the degree to which He could use me. See Appendix 1 for a list of prayers and practices that have been foundational to my life as a Spiritual Mountaineer.

Think about how much we assume about life and stability. We want safety above all. And I understand that feeling. But God is not safe; the Bible does not contain stories about people who achieved safety! The Bible gives us stories about those who risked everything, stepped into the jaws of death, were sawn in two, went to prison, and became mighty in war.

We have not been called to the safe and comfortable path. Those who will succeed us have certainly not been called to safety either. If you live in the real world, your health, your finances, and your career all confirm that. And if you're a parent, you know part of your job is prepare your offspring to face new threats and dangers. We must pass on the heart of a mountaineer.

For example, I know from long and intense experience, a big pharmaceutical company can hold very promising new medicines, something that can manage or cure a disease. But that medicine, that drug, takes the whole company, including the investors, out on a very thin ledge. A couple of adverse events in a clinical trial can shut down a billion-dollar project. Think of a small biotech company that has one technology. Maybe they've raised $10 million and everything hangs on a series of critical experiments; if one of those goes wonky, the whole thing unravels. I've seen it happen! It was so much like mountaineering; we were dancing along a very narrow thousand-foot cliff, with our toes over the edge. The difference between success and failure was a hairbreadth. Failure would be catastrophic.

In that situation, you ask yourself, "Okay, so what am I going to do about it?" It's like Apollo 13, "Failure is not an option." So, what do you do? You focus on what you can manage, what's controllable. You concentrate on what you could do *right now* to solve the immediate problem and you work the process.

What About You?

When I spoke with a friend several years ago about feeling a passion and pressure toward leadership, he simply said, "Take others with you." I've tried to do that. You might say that's why I wrote this book.

So what about you? Will you join me on a journey far beyond what you've ever dreamed? What dreams has God placed in your heart? What makes your heart pound?

We have no reason to be intimidated by, or fearful of, the world. As stewards of God, entrusted with His purpose, we can walk through the earth with the same power and authority as a massive oil tanker moving through the ocean. As instruments of God, we influence those across the landscape of our lives. Remember the earlier story of Leonardo da Vinci's brush he used to paint the Mona Lisa? It would be foolish to ascribe majesty to the brush. It was simply the instrument in the master's hand. So are we.

I believe we are destined to do greater things than Paul, Jesus, or any others who've gone before us. But we don't do that as individuals. Rather, as the church, His Body, we can and should impact the earth simply because we are part of His global Body! Two thousand years ago, Jesus discipled and commissioned 12 men. But the Holy Spirit has fanned that flame as it covered the earth. That carries much greater impact.

To fill up our part in His corporate Body, He calls us to live a fully developed human life, not just some slightly improved version of it. You and I carry the God of all creation around inside us. We can see with new eyes, think with new logic, reason with His mind, speak words of life, analyze problems from a different perspective, and reach conclusions based on God's wisdom. When we live in His Spirit, we should be better accountants, litigators, physicians, CEOs, maintenance technicians, hair stylists, or police officers than anyone in the world.

When we have emptied ourselves of all that is not of Him through the climb up the mountain, might we really see the Sovereign of all creation? As bearers of His image, we are called to reflect Him everywhere we go and to everyone we touch, to live Isaiah 58. I've found the backpacker's motto to be foundational: Leave everything better than you found it. To me, that included leaving *everyone* better than I found them.

The whole world desperately needs to see *real* people, living souls they can relate to in terms of the real struggles they face but who walk through them with peace, vision, faith, hope, and love that is beyond comprehension. They need the touch for those who carry the presence of God in their lives. That is what everyone hungers for.

Jesus came to bring heaven back to earth. What will the new heaven and new earth be like? No more misunderstandings, hidden agendas, guile, and deceit. No more battered self-esteem, no power brokers or egomaniacs.

Think about it; if we all lived in the rare and high-ground atmosphere of His Presence, in the Death Zone on a daily basis, the entire world would be different. The realms we now know as politics, education, entertainment, news media, and other professions and trades would reflect the values and glory of heaven. On earth. Maybe that's why Jesus taught us to pray, "Thy kingdom come on earth as it is in heaven."

In my world of business, I can only imagine what would happen if we were led with a stewardship mentality. Could *heaven-on-earth* provide goods and services which would benefit all of society? Could we also care for the poor? Imagine a day when we do that rather than waiting for the government to do it. If we dared to live as He outlined in His design of society, we would have no need for social security, welfare, government housing, or even insurance. Imagine living in a place of "Things which eye has not seen, and ear has not heard, and which have not entered into the heart of man, all that God has prepared for those who love Him." 1 Corinthians 2:9.

The Call

Do you want to go up where the air is thin and the climbing difficult, where few have ever traveled? Do you want to walk with God on the great peaks He has prepared for you? Do you want to taste that life now, not just someday in heaven? I believe He calls us to walk with Him "up there."

Maybe you feel the Spirit of God has been calling you all your life, trying to awaken a hunger for the pure air of the heights of the earth. Maybe you sense a call to climb the Mountain of God.

Will you be the Spiritual Mountaineer that God can use anytime, anywhere? He is not looking for superstars. As the Bible records in so many stories, He chooses simple earthen vessels, those who can handle the challenges of the mountain ranges and be available for Him whenever and however He chooses. God is looking for vessels He can use, often in seemingly impossible circumstances where we will execute fearlessly. He's been leading you to the place where He can say: "Now I've got something I can work with."

Just as God did with the Children of Israel, you may wander in the desert for as long as it takes for Him to purge "Egypt" from your identity. He told you about your Promised Land. Will you stay on the climb until you reach the summit? It may be thousands of feet above you, but as you walk out a surrendered life in true faith and trust in your Guide, you will make it.

Responding to the call may be the hardest thing you'll ever do. But He's waiting for you there. Press on, climber, press on, dig deep, refuse to quit. Trust me; the summit will ruin you for lesser things.

Once you stand there, you will wonder how you could have lived without reaching it.

••••••••••••••••••••••••

"To those who have struggled with them, the mountains reveal beauties they will not disclose to those who make no effort. That is the reward the mountains give to the effort. And it is because they have so much to give and give it so lavishly to those who will wrestle with them that men love the mountains and go back to them again and again… the mountains reserve their choice gifts for those who stand on their summits."
Sir Frances Younghusband

••••••••••••••••••••••••

APPENDICES

....

Appendix 1

Foundations for a Mountaineering Life

Prayer:

Over the years, I've noticed that a few prayers seem to flow over and over again from my heart. As such, they've proven to be foundational in setting the direction of my life. As they seem to invite God to shape who I am, I can see they might also help others to find a new voice for their prayers. These are more fully developed in the workbook, *Spiritual Mountaineering: Climbing Higher.*

- God, what's on Your mind and heart?
- Teach me how to pray so You can fully do what You need to do in and through me.
- Make me who You want me to be, even if I don't recognize what You are doing, and even if I resist Your hand.
- Do whatever it takes to keep me honest and humble before You.
- Do whatever it takes to keep me ever mindful of my desperate need for You and Your forgiveness.
- Give me ears to hear, eyes to see, and a heart that is willing to obey.

- Teach me to be truly honest with You, other people, and myself (Ps 139).
- Teach me what surrender is.
- Help me understand what a bond servant is.
- Teach me what a godly man, husband, and father is.
- Let Your grace and providence be over me, my family, and anyone who will affect my life.
- Give me the same love for Jesus that the Father has for Him.
- Give me the same love for the world that Jesus has.
- Pray Ephesians 1:15-21 and 3:14-19

Fundamental Bond Servant Principles:

It seems that many Christians today never fully grasp the scope and importance of the critical foundational points of walking with God. Through both His kindness and severity to me (Romans 11:22), I've learned to press God on each of the points below. I want to know what God requires of those who walk with Him on the mountaintop. I want to understand how He works through us. What impedes His work with His people?

Ask Him to show you how He wants to apply these to your life.

- **The magnitude of His love.** Most of us never understand the breadth, depth, and profound intimacy of His love is for us. His love removes all fear and the impulses for performance and comparison. It is the only thing that makes us free in every respect (read The Song of Solomon 4:9 and Zephaniah 3:17).
- **Honesty.** What does it mean to be absolutely honest with ourselves and with God? I must recognize and be comfortable with who I am and who I am not, what I'm good at, and what

I'm not good at. In view of Psalm 139, is it possible to hide anything from Him? So, why do we try? And if we understand His love for us, why do we ever know shame (Heb 4:13)?

- **Surrender.** What does it mean to own nothing, have no rights, hold no basis for expectations, and therefore carry no disappointment or offense? It means to be a bondservant and be totally dead to self.
- **Hearing His Voice.** Because Jesus said He only did what the Father told Him to do, we should see that a clear sense of hearing is vitally important. We must train our ears to hear the still small voice in hurricane-force winds and firestorms.
- **What if He really set you free?** Most of us have never fully grasped what complete freedom means. What if you had no emotional baggage or wounds, no financial constraints, no limitations on your energy or time, no physical constraints? What would you do? As author Robert Farrar Capon asked, "What would you do with freedom if you had it?"
- **Generational Succession.** When God gave David the dream to build the temple, He didn't mean for David to build it. That job was for his son, Solomon. I tend to fixate on "God's call for my life," but rarely understand that God's execution timeframe is much, much longer than the span of my life. He calls us to collectively build a foundation that succeeding generations can stand on and build further for successive generations.
- **Spiritual Inertia and Cause and Effect.** We can clearly see by God's word and Jesus' example that discipline and devotion set the stage for a life aligned with God. They shape the life that He can work with. The inertia of a devotional life is pivotal for sustaining us through the hard push to the summit. It will keep us going when we are exhausted, unable to eat,

and pushing through pain. It also helps maintain our spiritual perimeter defenses. I see a cause and effect dynamic at work; a solid devotional life often seems to invite God's grace and sustaining power.

There is a negative cause and effect as well. By neglecting our devotional life, we invite Satan's attack. He will use our sin and weaknesses as an entry point to attack and undermine what seems like unrelated areas of our lives. Although the secondary attack often comes because we gave him access, he keeps us from seeing the correlation between the two; he disguises cause and effect.

Appendix 2

Devotional Reading:

These verses have been foundational for me over the years; I hope you find them useful. This resource is more developed in the workbook, *Spiritual Mountaineering: Climbing Higher.*

Exodus 23: 20-33	Isaiah 58: 4-14
Leviticus 10: 1-11	Micah 2: 13
Joshua 1: 7-9	Micah 6: 8
Joshua 14: 12	Habakkuk 2: 1-3
Judges 2:15-23	Zechariah 3: 1-7
2 Kings 6:16-17	Romans 13: 11-14
2 Chronicles 29: 11	2 Corinthians 10: 3-5
Psalms 1, 15, 24, and 139	Galatians 4: 1-5
Psalms 19:12-14	Ephesians 1: 15-23
Psalms 60: 4	Ephesians 3: 14-21
Psalms 90: 16,17	Philippians 4: 6-8
Psalms 105: 16-22	Philippians 4: 11-13
Psalms 121	Colossians 4: 5-6
Proverbs 3	Hebrews 12
Proverbs 11: 23-30	James 1: 2-8
Isaiah 45:1-8	

AUTHOR BIO

....

JIM MONSOR HAS BEEN ACTIVE in the biotech and pharmaceutical industry, church, and non-profit leadership for nearly forty years. He is a founder and CEO of Relay Life Science, an early stage pharmaceutical company developing a compound with the potential to treat major neurodegenerative disorders. Jim also serves as the CEO of NuLine Sensors, LLC. In addition, he leads a statewide mentor program which coaches life science entrepreneurs for the State of Tennessee and is actively involved in an inner city entrepreneur mentorship program. Jim has been married to Beth for 35 years. Together, they have raised four adult daughters. The Monsor family lives in Franklin, Tennessee. *Spiritual Mountaineering* is his first book.